Healthier Food C

Use this fat gram comparison to help you make he

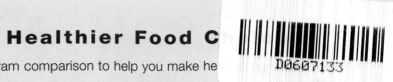

Item	Amount		Fat	Calories (% from Fat)
Whole milk	8	ounces	7.3g	138 (48%)
Reduced-fat milk	8	ounces	4.3g	113 (34%)
Fat-free milk	8	ounces	0.4g	79 (5%)
Whipping cream	2	tablespoons	11.0g	103 (96%)
Half-and-half	2	tablespoons	3.7g	43 (77%)
Evaporated skimmed milk	2	tablespoons	0.1g	25 (4%)
Egg, whole	1	large	5.2g	77 (61%)
Egg whites	2	large	0.0g	32 (0%)
Egg substitute, fat-free	¼	cup (1 egg)	0.0g	30 (0%)
Butter	1	tablespoon	11.5g	102 (100%)
Margarine	1	tablespoon	11.4g	101 (100%)
Light butter	1	tablespoon	6.0g	50 (100%)
Reduced-calorie margarine	1	tablespoon	5.6g	50 (100%)
Cream cheese	1	ounce	9.9g	99 (90%)
Neufchâtel cheese	1	ounce	6.6g	74 (80%)
Nonfat cream cheese	1	ounce	0.0g	25 (0%)
Cheddar cheese	1	ounce	9.4g	114 (74%)
Reduced-fat Cheddar cheese	1	ounce	4.5g	80 (51%)
Nonfat Cheddar cheese	1	ounce	0.0g	40 (0%)
Sour cream	1	tablespoon	3.0g	31 (87%)
Reduced-fat sour cream	1	tablespoon	1.0g	18 (50%)
Nonfat sour cream	1	tablespoon	0.0g	8 (0%)
Mayonnaise	1	tablespoon	10.9g	99 (99%)
Reduced-fat mayonnaise	1	tablespoon	4.6g	44 (94%)
Nonfat mayonnaise	1	tablespoon	0.0g	12 (0%)
Pork sausage	1	ounce	11.4g	118 (87%)
Turkey breakfast sausage	1	ounce	3.5g	52 (61%)
Bacon	1	slice, cooked	5.7g	64 (80%)
Turkey bacon	1	slice, cooked	2.5g	34 (66%)
Canadian bacon	1	slice, cooked	2.0g	43 (42%)

**Fresh Strawberries
with Lime Custard**
(recipe, page 42)

Teriyaki Turkey Burger
(recipe, page 170)

Mexican-Style Poached Eggs
(recipe, page 73)

Vegetable-Tortellini Salad
(recipe, page 143)

Weight Watchers.

Quick, Light & Healthy

Cookbook

Oxmoor House.

Library of Congress Catalog Card Number: 98-65613
ISBN: 0-8487-1690-6

Manufactured in the United States of America
First Printing 1998

Be sure to check with your health-care provider before making any changes in your diet.

Weight Watchers is a registered trademark of Weight Watchers International, Inc., and is used under license by Healthy Living, Inc.

Editor-in-Chief: Nancy Fitzpatrick Wyatt
Senior Foods Editor: Katherine M. Eakin
Senior Editor, Editorial Services: Olivia Kindig Wells
Art Director: James Boone

Weight Watchers Quick, Light & Healthy Cookbook

Editor: Kate Matuszak Wheeler, R.D.
Associate Art Director: Cynthia R. Cooper
Designer: Clare T. Minges
Copy Editor: Keri Bradford Anderson
Editorial Assistant: Catherine S. Ritter
Proofreader: Kathryn Stroud
Director, Test Kitchens: Kathleen Royal Phillips
Assistant Director, Test Kitchens: Gayle Hayes Sadler
Test Kitchens Staff: Susan Hall Bellows, Julie Christopher, Michele Fuller, Caroline A. Grant, Becky Hay,
    Natalie E. King, Elizabeth Tyler Luckett, Andee Noble, Iris Crawley O'Brien, Jan A. Smith
Photographer: Brit Huckabay
Photo Stylist: Virginia Cravens
Publishing Systems Administrator: Rick Tucker
Production and Distribution Director: Phillip Lee
Associate Production Manager: Vanessa Cobbs Richardson
Production Assistant: Faye Porter Bonner

Cover: Twenty-Minute Chili, page 76
Back Cover: Pineapple-Coconut Shortcakes, page 44

CONTENTS

Introduction

Quick Cooking Basics......................................8

About These Recipes..................................10

Quick, Light & Healthy Recipes

Appetizers & Beverages........................11

Breads...25

Desserts.. 41

Fish & Shellfish..................................... 55

Meatless Main Dishes............................71

Meats.. 89

Poultry... 109

Salads... 131

Sides.. 145

Soups & Sandwiches...........................161

Make-Ahead Recipes..........................177

Recipe Index.. 189

Acknowledgments & Credits......................... 192

Quick Cooking Basics

Weight Watchers Quick, Light & Healthy Cookbook gives you recipes with short ingredient lists, easy-to-find ingredients, and numbered steps. Put these recipes on the table fast using a few quick cooking basics.

First, **stock your pantry** with a variety of basic ingredients. Use the chart below as a guide for staple items to keep on hand; then shop for fresh ingredients as you need them.

Second, **equip your kitchen** for fast cooking using the facing chart. Preparing and cooking healthy foods quickly is easy when you have the right equipment.

Third, **shop wisely.** Buy ingredients in the closest-to-usable form. You'll pay a little more for the convenience, but when your goal is to cook quickly, it's worth it. For more shopping tips, read the facing page.

Stock Your Pantry

Choose nonfat, low-fat, reduced-fat, reduced-sodium, or no-salt-added products.

Baking Supplies
Canned evaporated milk
Cherry pie filling
Graham cracker crust
Semisweet chocolate morsels
Sweetened condensed milk

Breads
Biscuit and baking mix
Flour tortillas
Frozen bread dough
Submarine rolls
Whole wheat hamburger buns
Whole wheat pita rounds

Broths and Soups
Canned beef and chicken broths
Canned soups

Condiments and Seasonings
Fruit spread
Garlic
Hoisin sauce
Horseradish sauce
Hot sauce

Mayonnaise
Mustards
Peanut butter
Salad dressings
Salsa
Soy sauce/teriyaki sauce
Vinegars
Worcestershire sauce

Eggs and Dairy
Eggs/egg substitute
Buttermilk
Cheese
Dry milk powder
Frozen whipped topping
Grated Parmesan cheese
Milk
Process cream cheese
Sour cream
Yogurt

Fruits and Vegetables
Assorted canned fruits in juice
Assorted canned vegetables
Assorted frozen vegetable
  seasoning blends

Canned green chiles
Canned tomatoes: whole,
  diced, stewed, chili-style
Dried tomatoes
Frozen or canned fruit juices
Frozen vegetable soup mix
Roasted red pepper in water
Spaghetti sauce
Tomato paste

Herbs and Spices
Basil
Caraway seeds
Chili powder
Cinnamon
Creole seasoning blend
Garlic powder
Lemon-pepper seasoning

Beans, Grains, and Pastas
Beans: black, garbanzo,
  kidney, white
Grains: couscous, quick-
  cooking rice
Pastas: variety of shapes
  and sizes

Equip Your Kitchen

Cook with speed using these handy tools.

Assorted utensils: kitchen scissors, pizza
    cutter, rubber spatulas, vegetable peeler,
    wire whisk, and wooden spoons
Broiler pan with rack
Colander
Dutch oven
Food processor/mini-chopper
Hand mixer
Instant-read meat thermometer
Jellyroll pan
Knives: good quality chef's, paring, and slicing

Measuring cups: dry and liquid
Measuring spoons
Microwave oven
Mixing bowls (assorted sizes)
Nonstick baking pans, saucepans, and
    skillets
Skillets: 8-inch cast-iron and 10-inch
    ovenproof
Steam basket or steamer
Wire grilling basket
Wok or stir-fry pan

Shop Wisely

Practice these tips to streamline your shopping and cook healthy in a hurry.

○ Plan weekly menus. Begin by taking inventory of your pantry, refrigerator, and freezer; then plan meals around what you have on hand, including leftovers. Fill in with new recipes when possible.

○ Maintain an orderly refrigerator. It saves time and cuts down on wasted food. Keep most often used items up front and in the door racks. Clean and reorganize every few weeks.

○ Buy ready-to-use ingredients. Select skinned, boned chicken breast halves, shredded cheese, jarred minced garlic,

roasted red peppers, refrigerated pastas, packaged cut vegetables, and bags of washed lettuce and shredded cabbage.

○ Check out salad bars for cut fruits and vegetables, cooked pastas, and shredded cheeses. Look to the deli or meat counter for cooked chicken or shrimp. You can buy the amount you need and save money by avoiding waste.

○ Buy frozen vegetables such as peas, spinach, or corn, and frozen mixed vegetable blends instead of fresh vegetables to reduce preparation time.

About These Recipes

Weight Watchers® Quick, Light & Healthy Cookbook gives you the nutrition facts you want to know. To make your life easier, we've provided the following useful information with every recipe:

- Diabetic exchange values for those who use them as a guide for planning meals
- A number calculated through **POINTS®** Food System, an integral part of *Weight Watchers* **1•2•3 Success**™ Weight Loss Plan
- A complete nutrient analysis per serving

Diabetic Exchanges

Exchange values are provided for people who use them for calorie-controlled diets and for people with diabetes. All foods within a certain group contain approximately the same amount of nutrients and calories, so one serving of a food from a food group can be substituted or exchanged for one serving of any other item on the list.

The food groups are meat, starch, vegetable, fruit, fat, and milk. The exchange values are based on the *Exchange Lists for Meal Planning* developed by the American Diabetes Association and The American Dietetic Association.

POINTS Food System

Every recipe also includes a number assigned through **POINTS.** This system uses a formula based on the calorie, fat, and fiber content of the food. Foods with more calories and fat (like a slice of pepperoni pizza) receive high numbers, while fruits and vegetables receive low numbers. For more information about the numbers assigned through **POINTS,** the **1•2•3**

Success Weight Loss Plan, and the *Weight Watchers* meeting nearest you, call 1-800-651-6000.

Nutritional Analyses

Each recipe offers a complete listing of nutrients; the numbers in the list are based on the following assumptions:

- Unless otherwise indicated, meat, poultry, and fish refer to skinned, boned, and cooked servings.
- When we give a range for an ingredient (3 to 3½ cups flour, for instance), we calculate using the lesser amount.
- Some alcohol calories evaporate during heating; the analysis reflects that.
- Only the amount of marinade absorbed by the food is used in calculation.
- Garnishes and optional ingredients are not included in the analysis.

The nutritional values used in our calculations either come from a computer program by Computrition, Inc., or are provided by food manufacturers.

appetizers
&
beverages

Blue Cheese-Bean Dip

PREP: 5 minutes   **COOK:** 6 minutes

Exchange
Free

POINTS
0

Per Serving
17 Calories
2.1g Carbohydrate
0.4g Fat (0.3g saturated)
0.3g Fiber
1.0g Protein
1mg Cholesterol
52mg Sodium
16mg Calcium
0.2mg Iron

⅓ cup evaporated skimmed milk
½ teaspoon dried thyme
½ teaspoon freshly ground pepper
¼ teaspoon ground sage
¼ teaspoon salt
2 (15-ounce) cans cannellini beans, rinsed and drained
2 cloves garlic, sliced
2 ounces crumbled blue cheese
1 tablespoon grated Parmesan cheese
Vegetable cooking spray
½ cup soft breadcrumbs, toasted
2 tablespoons chopped fresh parsley

1. Position knife blade in food processor bowl; add first 7 ingredients. Process until smooth; stir in cheeses.

2. Spoon bean mixture into a shallow 1-quart baking dish coated with cooking spray. Cover with heavy-duty plastic wrap, and vent; microwave at HIGH 6 minutes, stirring every 2 minutes.

3. Combine breadcrumbs and parsley; sprinkle over bean mixture. Serve dip with Melba toast rounds, pita wedges, or no-oil-baked tortilla chips. Yield: 3 cups (1 tablespoon per serving).

Make ½ cup **soft breadcrumbs** by tearing 1 slice of fresh or slightly stale sandwich bread into small pieces. To toast breadcrumbs for this recipe, place them on a baking sheet; broil 5½ inches from heat (with electric oven door partially opened) 2 minutes, stirring occasionally.

Roasted Red Pepper and Onion Dip

PREP: 11 minutes   COOK: 10 minutes

1½ cups sliced purple onion (about 1½ purple onions)
2   cloves garlic
1   (12-ounce) jar roasted sweet red peppers, drained and coarsely
        chopped (or 3 large roasted red peppers, chopped)
¼   cup fine, dry breadcrumbs
3   tablespoons plain nonfat yogurt
1   tablespoon red wine vinegar
1   teaspoon olive oil
¼   teaspoon salt
⅛   teaspoon hot sauce

Exchange
Free

POINTS
0

Per Serving
12 Calories
2.1g Carbohydrate
0.3g Fat (0.0g saturated)
0.3g Fiber
0.4g Protein
0mg Cholesterol
28mg Sodium
8mg Calcium
0.1mg Iron

1. Place onion and garlic on an aluminum foil-lined baking sheet; broil 5½ inches from heat (with electric oven door partially opened) 10 minutes. Let stand 5 minutes.

2. Position knife blade in food processor bowl; add onion, garlic, and chopped red pepper. Process mixture until finely chopped. Add breadcrumbs and remaining ingredients to processor bowl; process until smooth. Serve with pita wedges, low-fat crackers, or raw fresh vegetables. Yield: 2 cups (1 tablespoon per serving).

Roast peppers for this recipe by following these 3 simple steps:
1. Cut 3 large red peppers in half; remove seeds and membranes. Place the peppers, skin side up, on a baking sheet; press each with the palm of your hand to flatten.
2. Broil 5½ inches from heat 15 to 20 minutes or until charred. Plunge the charred peppers into a bowl of ice water.
3. Peel and discard the skins from the cooled peppers. Then coarsely chop the roasted pepper to use in this recipe.

Three-Bean Artichoke Dip

PREP: 8 minutes

Exchange
½ Starch

POINTS
1

Per Serving
46 Calories
8.0g Carbohydrate
0.6g Fat (0.1g saturated)
1.6g Fiber
2.8g Protein
0mg Cholesterol
109mg Sodium
21mg Calcium
0.8mg Iron

1   (15-ounce) can black beans, rinsed and drained
1   (15-ounce) can red kidney beans, rinsed and drained
1   (15-ounce) can navy beans, rinsed and drained
1   (14-ounce) can artichoke hearts, drained and finely chopped
⅓   cup red wine vinegar
¼   cup chopped purple onion (about ½ purple onion)
2   tablespoons sliced ripe olives
2   tablespoons lemon juice
1½ teaspoons dried basil
2   teaspoons roasted garlic-flavored vegetable oil (or 2 teaspoons olive oil plus 1 clove garlic, minced)

1. Combine all ingredients in a medium bowl, stirring mixture well. Serve immediately; or cover dip, and chill until ready to serve. Serve dip with no-oil-baked tortilla chips or Melba toast rounds. Yield: 6 cups (¼ cup per serving).

Need a quick **main-dish salad?** Just place 1 cup bean mixture on your favorite leaf lettuce for a flavorful, high-fiber meal. And you'll enjoy it even more knowing that this single serving has only 183 calories and a mere 3 points.

Spinach con Queso

PREP: 8 minutes   COOK: 20 minutes

1   (10-ounce) package frozen chopped spinach, thawed
1   (8-ounce) package nonfat cream cheese, softened
1   cup (4 ounces) shredded reduced-fat sharp Cheddar cheese
¼   cup evaporated skimmed milk
2   teaspoons 40%-less-sodium taco seasoning mix
1   (10-ounce) can diced tomatoes and green chiles, drained
Vegetable cooking spray

1. Drain spinach well, pressing between layers of paper towels to remove excess moisture.

2. Place cream cheese in a large bowl, mash with a fork until smooth. Add spinach, Cheddar cheese, and next 3 ingredients; stir well. Spoon into a 1-quart baking dish coated with cooking spray.

3. Bake at 400° for 20 minutes or until mixture is bubbly. Serve dip with no-oil-baked tortilla chips, low-fat crackers, or Melba toast rounds. Yield: 2½ cups (1 tablespoon per serving).

Exchange
Free

POINTS
0

Per Serving
18 Calories
0.9g Carbohydrate
0.6g Fat (0.3g saturated)
0.2g Fiber
2.0g Protein
3mg Cholesterol
84mg Sodium
51mg Calcium
0.2mg Iron

Mediterranean Nachos

PREP: 18 minutes COOK: 5 minutes

Exchange
½ Starch

POINTS
0

Per Serving
32 Calories
5.7g Carbohydrate
0.6g Fat (0.1g saturated)
1.4g Fiber
1.0g Protein
0mg Cholesterol
76mg Sodium
11mg Calcium
0.4mg Iron

2   (6-inch) pita bread rounds
Vegetable cooking spray
¼   teaspoon salt
1   (15-ounce) can garbanzo beans, drained
¼   cup sliced green onions (about 2 green onions)
2   tablespoons lemon juice
1   tablespoon fat-free milk
1   teaspoon olive oil
2   cloves garlic
1   cup chopped tomato (about 1 medium tomato)
3   tablespoons chopped ripe olives

1. Separate each pita bread round into 2 rounds; cut each round into 6 wedges. Place wedges on a large baking sheet; coat wedges with cooking spray, and sprinkle evenly with salt. Bake at 450° for 5 minutes or until lightly browned.

2. Meanwhile, position knife blade in food processor bowl; add beans and next 5 ingredients. Process until smooth, stopping once to scrape down sides.

3. Spread 2 teaspoons bean mixture over each pita wedge; sprinkle wedges evenly with chopped tomato and olives. Serve nachos immediately. Yield: 24 appetizers (1 per serving).

The easiest way to **cut pita bread** into wedges is with a pizza cutter or kitchen shears.

Polenta Bites with Red Pepper Sauce (photo, page 22)

PREP: 18 minutes   COOK: 10 minutes

¼   cup dried tomatoes (packed without oil)
½   cup hot water
1   (16-ounce) package refrigerated polenta
Vegetable cooking spray
⅓   cup Italian-seasoned breadcrumbs
1   tablespoon grated Parmesan cheese, divided
1   (12-ounce) jar roasted sweet red peppers, drained
1   tablespoon balsamic vinegar
2   teaspoons sugar

1. Combine tomatoes and hot water; let stand 5 minutes. Drain.

2. Slice polenta into 8 equal slices; cut each slice into fourths. Coat polenta pieces with cooking spray. Place breadcrumbs and 1 teaspoon Parmesan cheese in a heavy-duty, zip-top plastic bag. Place 8 polenta pieces in bag; shake well, and remove polenta from bag. Repeat with remaining polenta. Place on an ungreased baking sheet.

3. Broil 5½ inches from heat (with electric oven door partially opened) 10 to 12 minutes or until lightly browned, turning polenta after 5 minutes.

4. Meanwhile, place tomatoes, red peppers, vinegar, and sugar in container of an electric blender; cover and process until smooth, stopping once to scrape down sides. Spoon mixture into a small microwave-safe bowl; stir in remaining 2 teaspoons Parmesan cheese. Microwave at HIGH 2 minutes.

5. To serve, place polenta bites on a serving tray around heated sauce. Serve with wooden picks. Yield: 8 servings (4 polenta bites and 2½ tablespoons sauce per serving).

Exchange
1 Starch

POINTS
1

Per Serving
83 Calories
16.0g Carbohydrate
0.4g Fat (0.2g saturated)
1.4g Fiber
2.3g Protein
0mg Cholesterol
303mg Sodium
14mg Calcium
0.3mg Iron

Find ready-to-serve **polenta** in the produce section of your grocery store (it comes in a tube).

Open-Faced Hawaiian Pork Rolls

PREP: 5 minutes   COOK: 23 minutes

Exchanges
1 Lean Meat
½ Starch

POINTS
2

Per Serving
93 Calories
9.2g Carbohydrate
3.2g Fat (1.5g saturated)
0.6g Fiber
6.5g Protein
22mg Cholesterol
191mg Sodium
12mg Calcium
0.1mg Iron

2   (¾-pound) teriyaki-flavored pork tenderloins (such as Hormel)
¾   cup light process cream cheese
¼   cup low-sugar orange marmalade, divided
3   tablespoons chopped green onions, divided (about 1 green onion)
2   tablespoons flaked coconut, toasted and divided
¾   teaspoon curry powder
1   (12-ounce) package Hawaiian rolls

1. Line a 13- x 9- x 2-inch pan with aluminum foil; place pork in pan. Bake at 425° for 23 to 25 minutes or until a meat thermometer inserted into thickest portion registers 160°, turning pork once during baking.

2. Meanwhile, combine cream cheese, 2 tablespoons marmalade, 1½ tablespoons green onions, 1 tablespoon coconut, and curry powder; stir mixture well.

3. Slice unseparated rolls in half horizontally, using a serrated knife. Spread cream cheese mixture over cut side of rolls. Separate rolls into 24 pieces.

4. Slice pork into 48 (¼-inch-thick) slices. Place 2 slices on each roll half. Top with remaining 2 tablespoons marmalade, 1½ tablespoons onions, and 1 tablespoon coconut. Yield: 24 appetizers (1 per serving).

Spread the **cream cheese mixture** on the rolls before you separate them into 24 pieces. It'll save you some time.

Lemonade-Mint Iced Tea

PREP: 17 minutes

8   cups water, divided
12 regular-size mint-flavored tea bags
1½ tablespoons sugar-free lemon-flavored soft drink mix
Fresh mint sprigs (optional)

1. Bring 4 cups water to a boil in a saucepan. Remove from heat; add tea bags. Cover and steep 7 minutes. Remove and discard tea bags.

2. Pour tea into a large pitcher; add soft drink mix and remaining 4 cups water, stirring well. Serve over ice. Garnish with mint, if desired. Yield: 8 cups (1 cup per serving).

Lemon-mint ice cubes will enhance the flavor of this tea. Simply place a small mint sprig and lemon slice in each section of ice cube trays; add water. Freeze until firm.

Exchange
Free

POINTS
0

Per Serving
7 Calories
0.7g Carbohydrate
0.0g Fat (0.0g saturated)
0.0g Fiber
0.0g Protein
0mg Cholesterol
7mg Sodium
0mg Calcium
0.0mg Iron

Sunrise Slush (photo, opposite page)

PREP: 8 minutes

Exchanges
2 Fruit

POINTS
2

½ (12-ounce) container frozen orange-strawberry-banana juice
concentrate
1 (6-ounce) can unsweetened pineapple juice
3 cups ice cubes

Per Serving
121 Calories
28.4g Carbohydrate
0.0g Fat (0.0g saturated)
0.0g Fiber
0.9g Protein
0mg Cholesterol
23mg Sodium
7mg Calcium
0.1mg Iron

1. Combine all ingredients in container of an electric blender; cover and process until smooth, stopping once to scrape down sides. Serve immediately. Yield: 4 cups (1 cup per serving).

Frozen juice concentrate used in small amounts can add bright, intense flavor to recipes. Just scoop out the frozen amount you need. Reseal the container, and return the rest of the juice concentrate to the freezer for later use.

Blueberry Smoothie
(recipe, opposite page)

Polenta Bites with Red Pepper Sauce
(recipe, page 17)

Blueberry Smoothie (photo, opposite page)

PREP: 8 minutes

1   cup vanilla low-fat yogurt
½   cup grape juice
1½ cups fresh blueberries
1½ cups quartered fresh strawberries

1. Combine yogurt and grape juice in container of an electric blender; cover and process until blended. Add fruit; cover and process until smooth. Serve immediately. Yield: 4 cups (1 cup per serving).

Substitute your favorite fruits for the blueberries and strawberries in this simple, nutritious smoothie—the flavor combinations are unlimited.

Exchanges
½ Starch
1 Fruit

POINTS
2

Per Serving
119 Calories
25.4g Carbohydrate
1.1g Fat (0.5g saturated)
4.1g Fiber
3.5g Protein
3mg Cholesterol
43mg Sodium
113mg Calcium
0.4mg Iron

Mocha Cocoa Mix

PREP: 15 minutes

Exchanges

1 Starch

½ Skim Milk

POINTS

2

Per Serving

120 Calories

17.3g Carbohydrate

0.5g Fat (0.3g saturated)

0.1g Fiber

5.9g Protein

3mg Cholesterol

73mg Sodium

174mg Calcium

0.7mg Iron

1¾ cups instant nonfat dry milk powder

1 cup sifted powdered sugar

½ cup unsweetened cocoa

½ cup Swiss chocolate-flavored fat-free powdered nondairy coffee creamer

½ teaspoon ground cinnamon

½ cup instant coffee granules

1. Combine all ingredients; stir well. Store in an airtight container. To serve, place 3 tablespoons mix in a mug or cup. Add ¾ cup boiling water, stirring well. Yield: 3 cups mix, 16 servings (¾ cup per serving).

Mocha Cocoa Shake: Combine 2 tablespoons cocoa mix, ⅔ cup vanilla nonfat ice cream, and ⅓ cup fat-free milk in container of an electric blender; cover and process until smooth. Yield: 1 cup. Exchanges: 1½ Starch, 1 Skim Milk; Points: 5; Calories: 228

breads

Apple Butter-Bran Muffins

PREP: 5 minutes   **COOK:** 10 minutes

Exchanges
2 Starch
1 Fat

POINTS
3

Per Serving
174 Calories
31.8g Carbohydrate
4.7g Fat (1.0g saturated)
2.8g Fiber
2.5g Protein
28mg Cholesterol
212mg Sodium
11mg Calcium
0.4mg Iron

1   (7.4-ounce) package honey bran muffin mix
½   cup apple butter
⅓   cup chopped dates
1   tablespoon fat-free milk
1   egg, lightly beaten
Vegetable cooking spray

1. Combine first 5 ingredients, stirring just until dry ingredients are moistened. Spoon batter into muffin pans coated with cooking spray, filling three-fourths full.

2. Bake at 450° for 10 to 12 minutes or until lightly browned. Remove from pans immediately. Yield: 8 muffins (1 muffin per serving).

This fruit butter has no fat. Apple butter is actually thick preserves made of apples, sugar, spices, and cider. It adds moisture and sweet apple flavor to these muffins.

Bacon-Cheese Drop Biscuits (photo, page 40)

PREP: 10 minutes   COOK: 11 minutes

2   slices turkey bacon
2   cups reduced-fat biscuit and baking mix (such as Bisquick)
½   cup (2 ounces) shredded reduced-fat sharp Cheddar cheese
2   tablespoons chopped green onions
⅛   teaspoon ground red pepper
¾   cup fat-free milk
Vegetable cooking spray

1. Place bacon on a microwave-safe plate lined with paper towels. Microwave at HIGH 1½ minutes. Crumble bacon.

2. Combine bacon, biscuit mix, and next 3 ingredients, stirring mixture well. Add milk, stirring just until dry ingredients are moistened. Drop dough by rounded tablespoonfuls, 2 inches apart, onto a large baking sheet coated with cooking spray.

3. Bake at 400° 10 to 12 minutes or until golden. Serve immediately. Yield: 16 biscuits (1 biscuit per serving).

Exchange

1 Starch

POINTS

2

Per Serving

75 Calories

11.3g Carbohydrate

1.9g Fat (0.7g saturated)

0.0g Fiber

2.8g Protein

4mg Cholesterol

229mg Sodium

49mg Calcium

0.1mg Iron

An ounce of **turkey bacon** has two-thirds less fat than an ounce of regular bacon.

Cinnamon-Raisin Biscuits

PREP: 12 minutes   COOK: 10 minutes

Exchange

1 Starch

POINTS

2

Per Serving

89 Calories

17.0g Carbohydrate

1.7g Fat (0.3g saturated)

0.5g Fiber

1.7g Protein

0mg Cholesterol

55mg Sodium

46mg Calcium

0.7mg Iron

A good **biscuit dough** will be slightly sticky to the touch and should be kneaded gently just a few times.

1¾ cups all-purpose flour

2 teaspoons baking powder

⅓ cup raisins

2 tablespoons sugar

1¼ teaspoons ground cinnamon

⅔ cup nonfat buttermilk

2 tablespoons vegetable oil

Vegetable cooking spray

½ cup sifted powdered sugar

2 tablespoons unsweetened apple juice

1. Combine first 5 ingredients in a large bowl; make a well in center of mixture. Combine buttermilk and oil; add to flour mixture, stirring just until dry ingredients are moistened.

2. Turn dough out onto work surface; knead 3 to 5 times. Roll dough to ½-inch thickness; cut into rounds with a 2-inch biscuit cutter. Place rounds on a baking sheet coated with cooking spray.

3. Bake at 425° for 10 minutes or until golden. Combine powdered sugar and apple juice, stirring mixture well; drizzle over warm biscuits. Yield: 1½ dozen (1 biscuit per serving).

Cream Cheese Biscuits (photo, page 40)

PREP: 10 minutes   COOK: 10 minutes

2	cups self-rising flour, divided
1	teaspoon sugar
½	(8-ounce) package Neufchâtel cheese, cut into small pieces
2	tablespoons reduced-calorie stick margarine
¼	cup plus 3 tablespoons fat-free milk
	Vegetable cooking spray

Exchanges
1 Starch
½ Fat

POINTS
2

Per Serving
97 Calories
14.2g Carbohydrate
3.2g Fat (1.4g saturated)
0.0g Fiber
2.8g Protein
6mg Cholesterol
279mg Sodium
76mg Calcium
0.9mg Iron

1. Sprinkle 1 tablespoon flour over work surface. Combine remaining flour and sugar in a bowl; stir well. Cut in cheese with a pastry blender until mixture resembles coarse meal. Cut in margarine until it forms small pieces. Add milk, stirring mixture just until dry ingredients are moistened.

2. Turn dough out onto work surface. Knead 4 or 5 times. Pat dough to ½-inch thickness; cut into rounds with a 2-inch biscuit cutter. Place rounds on a baking sheet coated with cooking spray.

3. Bake at 450° for 10 minutes or until biscuits are lightly browned. Yield: 14 biscuits (1 biscuit per serving).

"Tender," "flaky," and **"delicious"** were just a few of our enthusiastic responses to these biscuits, which received our highest rating.

Sweet Potato Scones

PREP: 12 minutes   COOK: 10 minutes

Exchanges
2 Starch

POINTS
3

Per Serving
138 Calories
28.0g Carbohydrate
1.6g Fat (0.3g saturated)
0.7g Fiber
2.6g Protein
0mg Cholesterol
289mg Sodium
25mg Calcium
0.6mg Iron

Look for canned whole **sweet potatoes** in your supermarket. Drain the potatoes, and then mash them to use in this recipe.

1½ cups reduced-fat biscuit and baking mix (such as Bisquick)
¼ cup raisins
1 tablespoon sugar
½ teaspoon grated orange rind
½ cup canned, mashed sweet potato
¼ cup fat-free milk
½ teaspoon vanilla extract
Vegetable cooking spray
1½ teaspoons sugar
⅛ teaspoon ground cinnamon

1. Combine first 4 ingredients in a large bowl. Combine sweet potato, milk, and vanilla; add to raisin mixture, stirring just until dry ingredients are moistened. (Dough will be sticky.)

2. With floured hands, gather dough into a ball; pat ball into a 7-inch circle on a baking sheet coated with cooking spray.

3. Cut dough into 8 wedges, cutting to, but not through, bottom of dough. Combine 1½ teaspoons sugar and cinnamon; sprinkle mixture over dough.

4. Bake at 450° for 10 minutes or until scones are lightly browned. Yield: 8 scones (1 scone per serving).

Light Mayonnaise Rolls

PREP: 5 minutes   COOK: 12 minutes

1   cup self-rising flour
3   tablespoons reduced-fat mayonnaise
½   cup fat-free milk
Vegetable cooking spray

1. Combine first 3 ingredients, stirring just until flour is moistened. Spoon batter into muffin pans coated with cooking spray, filling two-thirds full.

2. Bake at 425° for 12 minutes or until rolls are lightly browned. Remove from pans immediately. Yield: ½ dozen (1 roll per serving).

> You can use 1 cup **all-purpose flour** plus 1 teaspoon baking powder and ½ teaspoon salt in place of 1 cup self-rising flour.

Exchanges
1 Starch
½ Fat

POINTS
2

Per Serving
103 Calories
16.9g Carbohydrate
2.5g Fat (0.1g saturated)
0.0g Fiber
2.8g Protein
3mg Cholesterol
331mg Sodium
96mg Calcium
1.0mg Iron

Tomato-Parmesan Flatbread

PREP: 7 minutes   COOK: 15 minutes

Exchanges

1½ Starch

½ Fat

POINTS

3

Per Serving

129 Calories

20.8g Carbohydrate

2.1g Fat (0.0g saturated)

0.3g Fiber

4.3g Protein

0mg Cholesterol

393mg Sodium

3mg Calcium

0.1mg Iron

2   tablespoons dried tomato bits (packed without oil)

1½   tablespoons commercial fat-free Caesar Italian dressing

1   (11.3-ounce) can refrigerated dinner rolls

2   tablespoons grated garlic-herb Parmesan cheese blend

Vegetable cooking spray

1. Combine tomato bits and dressing in a small bowl; let mixture stand 5 minutes.

2. Meanwhile, remove roll dough from package; separate into rolls. Roll each piece into a 4-inch round.

3. Brush rounds evenly with tomato mixture, and sprinkle evenly with Parmesan cheese blend. Place rounds on a baking sheet coated with cooking spray. Bake at 375° for 15 minutes or until golden. Yield: 8 servings (1 flatbread per serving).

Make your own **garlic-herb Parmesan cheese** by combining 2 tablespoons regular grated Parmesan cheese, ½ teaspoon dried Italian seasoning, and ⅛ teaspoon garlic powder.

Peppered Pimiento Cheese Bread

PREP: 11 minutes   COOK: 8 minutes

¾ cup (3 ounces) shredded nonfat Cheddar and mozzarella
      cheese blend
½ cup nonfat mayonnaise
3   tablespoons chopped green onions (about 1 green onion)
2   tablespoons diced pimiento
½ teaspoon seasoned pepper
2   (3-ounce) submarine rolls, halved lengthwise

1. Combine first 5 ingredients, stirring well.

2. Cut each roll in half crosswise. Spread cheese mixture evenly over cut sides of rolls. Place rolls on a baking sheet; bake at 400° for 8 minutes or until cheese melts. Yield: 8 slices (1 slice per serving).

Exchange
1 Starch

POINTS
1

Per Serving
72 Calories
12.9g Carbohydrate
0.4g Fat (0.1g saturated)
0.6g Fiber
5.3g Protein
0mg Cholesterol
369mg Sodium
59mg Calcium
0.5mg Iron

Broccoli-Cheddar Crescents

PREP: 16 minutes   COOK: 11 minutes

Exchanges
1 Starch
1 Fat

POINTS
3

Per Serving
114 Calories
12.9g Carbohydrate
5.1g Fat (1.3g saturated)
0.4g Fiber
3.5g Protein
2mg Cholesterol
264mg Sodium
34mg Calcium
0.2mg Iron

¾   cup frozen chopped broccoli flowerets

3   tablespoons (¾ ounce) shredded reduced-fat Cheddar cheese

2   tablespoons nonfat cream cheese

¼   teaspoon garlic powder

⅛   teaspoon ground red pepper

1   (8-ounce) package refrigerated reduced-fat crescent dinner rolls

1. Place broccoli in a microwave-safe bowl; microwave broccoli at HIGH 3 minutes or until thawed.

2. Meanwhile, combine Cheddar cheese and next 3 ingredients, stirring well. Place thawed broccoli on paper towels, and squeeze to remove excess water; stir broccoli into cheese mixture.

3. Unroll dough; separate into 8 triangles. Spoon 1 heaping tablespoon broccoli mixture onto wide part of each crescent roll. Roll crescents according to package directions.

4. Place rolls, point sides down, on an ungreased baking sheet. Bake at 375° for 11 to 13 minutes or until golden. Serve immediately. Yield: 8 servings (1 crescent per serving).

Frozen vegetables such as broccoli and spinach lose water when thawed. This extra liquid can cause baked products to be soggy. To remove excess water, squeeze thawed vegetables between paper towels.

Strawberry-Almond Danish

PREP: 13 minutes   COOK: 10 minutes

¼   cup nonfat cream cheese
1   tablespoon sifted powdered sugar
⅛   teaspoon almond extract
1   (8-ounce) package refrigerated reduced-fat crescent dinner rolls
2   tablespoons no-sugar-added strawberry spread
⅓   cup plus 1 tablespoon sifted powdered sugar
2   teaspoons fat-free milk

1. Combine first 3 ingredients, stirring until smooth; set aside.

2. Unroll dough; separate into 8 triangles. Spoon 1 heaping teaspoon cream cheese mixture onto wide part of each crescent roll. Dollop strawberry spread evenly over cream cheese mixture. Roll crescents according to package directions, pinching ends of crescents.

3. Place rolls, point sides down, on a baking sheet lined with parchment paper. Bake at 375° for 10 minutes or until golden.

4. Combine ⅓ cup plus 1 tablespoon powdered sugar and milk; stir well. Drizzle over crescents. Yield: 8 servings (1 Danish per serving).

Exchanges
1 Starch
1 Fat

POINTS
3

Per Serving
135 Calories
19.9g Carbohydrate
4.5g Fat (1.0g saturated)
0.0g Fiber
3.2g Protein
1mg Cholesterol
279mg Sodium
24mg Calcium
0.1mg Iron

Kitchen parchment paper eliminates the need for greasing the baking sheet—so cleanup is easy. (And the paper is inexpensive.)

Raisin Bread French Toast (photo, page 39)

PREP: 2 minutes   **COOK:** 9 minutes

Exchanges
2 Starch

POINTS
3

Per Serving
171 Calories
33.4g Carbohydrate
1.5g Fat (0.3g saturated)
1.9g Fiber
6.8g Protein
2mg Cholesterol
243mg Sodium
66mg Calcium
1.2mg Iron

½ cup egg substitute
¼ cup fat-free milk
½ teaspoon vanilla extract
¼ teaspoon ground cinnamon
Vegetable cooking spray
8 slices cinnamon-raisin bread
2 teaspoons sifted powdered sugar
½ cup reduced-calorie syrup

1. Combine first 4 ingredients in a shallow bowl, stirring well.

2. Coat a large nonstick skillet with cooking spray; place skillet over medium heat until hot.

3. Dip bread slices into egg substitute mixture, coating sides well. Place 4 slices in skillet; cook 2 minutes on each side or until lightly browned. Remove from skillet; sprinkle with half of powdered sugar.

4. Repeat with remaining bread slices and sugar. Serve with syrup. Yield: 4 servings (2 slices bread and 2 tablespoons syrup per serving).

Keep **cinnamon-raisin bread** on hand for this no-fuss French toast. You can have this breakfast treat on the table in 11 minutes flat.

Banana Pancakes

PREP: 15 minutes   COOK: 12 minutes

1   cup all-purpose flour
1   tablespoon sugar
⅛   teaspoon salt
1   cup nonfat buttermilk
1   teaspoon baking soda
½   cup mashed ripe banana
½   cup egg substitute
1   tablespoon vegetable oil
Vegetable cooking spray

Exchanges
1½ Starch
½ Fat

POINTS
3

Per Serving
150 Calories
25.2g Carbohydrate
2.8g Fat (0.6g saturated)
1.2g Fiber
5.8g Protein
2mg Cholesterol
260mg Sodium
88mg Calcium
1.4mg Iron

1. Combine first 3 ingredients in a large bowl; make a well in center of mixture. Combine buttermilk and soda, stirring well; add banana, egg substitute, and oil, stirring well.

2. Add buttermilk mixture to flour mixture, stirring just until dry ingredients are moistened.

3. For each pancake, pour ¼ cup batter onto a hot griddle or skillet coated with cooking spray, spreading batter to a 4-inch circle. Cook until tops are bubbly and edges looked cooked; turn and cook other sides. Yield: 12 pancakes (2 pancakes per serving).

Chipotle Chile Cornbread (photo, opposite page)

PREP: 6 minutes   COOK: 23 minutes

Exchanges
1½ Starch
1 Fat

POINTS
4

Per Serving
159 Calories
24.4g Carbohydrate
5.3g Fat (1.1g saturated)
0.2g Fiber
4.5g Protein
29mg Cholesterol
446mg Sodium
151mg Calcium
1.9mg Iron

Vegetable cooking spray
2   cups self-rising buttermilk cornmeal mix
1   cup nonfat buttermilk
2   tablespoons vegetable oil
1   to 2 tablespoons chopped chipotle chile in adobo sauce (or
        ¼ teaspoon ground red pepper)
2   teaspoons sugar
1   egg, lightly beaten

1. Coat an 8-inch cast-iron skillet with cooking spray; place in a preheated 425° oven 5 minutes.

2. Combine cornmeal mix and remaining 5 ingredients in a large bowl, stirring just until dry ingredients are moistened. Pour batter into hot skillet. Bake at 425° for 23 to 25 minutes or until cornbread is golden. Yield: 8 servings (1 slice per serving).

You can use an **eight-inch square pan** instead of an eight-inch cast-iron skillet. Serve this spicy cornbread with your favorite soup or chili.

Chipotle Chile Cornbread
(recipe, opposite page)

Raisin Bread French Toast
(recipe, page 36)

Cream Cheese Biscuits (recipe, page 29) and
Bacon-Cheese Drop Biscuits (recipe, page 27)

desserts

Fresh Strawberries with Lime Custard (photo, page 1)

PREP: 15 minutes

Exchanges
1 Starch
1½ Fruit

POINTS
3

Per Serving
190 Calories
37.5g Carbohydrate
0.5g Fat (0.0g saturated)
3.3g Fiber
7.8g Protein
5mg Cholesterol
81mg Sodium
119mg Calcium
0.5mg Iron

1   (8-ounce) container nonfat sour cream
½   cup fat-free sweetened condensed milk
½   teaspoon grated lime rind
1½ tablespoons fresh lime juice (about 1 medium lime)
3   cups sliced fresh strawberries

1. Combine first 4 ingredients, stirring well.

2. Spoon ¼ cup lime custard into each of four 6-ounce custard cups or dessert dishes. Top each with ¾ cup strawberries. Top each serving with 2 tablespoons lime custard. Yield: 4 servings.

Substitute your favorite berry in this superquick delicious dessert. Use lemon or orange rind and juice instead of lime rind and juice, if desired.

Blueberry-Lemon Cheesecake Parfaits

PREP: 24 minutes

2	(8-ounce) cartons lemon low-fat yogurt
4	ounces light process cream cheese
2	tablespoons sifted powdered sugar
1½	cups frozen reduced-calorie whipped topping, thawed
½	cup reduced-fat graham cracker crumbs
1	cup fresh or frozen blueberries, thawed

1. Spoon yogurt onto several layers of heavy-duty paper towels; spread to ½-inch thickness. Let stand 5 minutes. Scrape yogurt from paper towels into a bowl, using a rubber spatula.

2. Add cream cheese and powdered sugar to yogurt, stirring with a wire whisk until smooth. Fold in whipped topping.

3. Spoon ¼ cup yogurt mixture into each of six 4-ounce parfait glasses. Sprinkle each with 1 tablespoon graham cracker crumbs. Spoon blueberries evenly over parfaits. Top each serving with ¼ cup yogurt mixture and 1 teaspoon crumbs. Serve immediately; or cover and chill until ready to serve. Yield: 6 servings.

To make ½ cup reduced-fat **graham cracker crumbs,** place 4 whole graham crackers sheets (16 crackers) in a heavy-duty, zip-top plastic bag. Crush with a rolling pin or meat mallet.

Exchanges

2 Starch

1 Fat

POINTS

4

Per Serving

205 Calories

30.0g Carbohydrate

6.9g Fat (4.9g saturated)

1.2g Fiber

6.5g Protein

16mg Cholesterol

232mg Sodium

46mg Calcium

0.3mg Iron

Pineapple-Coconut Shortcakes (photo, page 59)

PREP: 15 minutes   **COOK:** 8 minutes

Exchanges
2 Starch
1 Fruit
1 Fat

POINTS
6

Per Serving
255 Calories
46.4g Carbohydrate
6.0g Fat (2.0g saturated)
0.3g Fiber
4.1g Protein
0mg Cholesterol
515mg Sodium
50mg Calcium
0.6mg Iron

To toast coconut, place coconut in a tray on a rack of a toaster oven, and bake 3 minutes or until lightly browned, stirring once.

2   cups reduced-fat biscuit and baking mix (such as Bisquick)
½   cup fat-free milk
2   tablespoons reduced-calorie margarine, melted
½   teaspoon vanilla extract
Vegetable cooking spray
1   (15¼-ounce) can pineapple tidbits in juice, undrained
2   tablespoons brown sugar
2   teaspoons cornstarch
¼   cup plus 2 tablespoons frozen reduced-calorie whipped topping, thawed
1   tablespoon flaked coconut, toasted

1. Place biscuit mix in a large bowl. Combine milk, margarine, and vanilla; add to dry ingredients, stirring just until dry ingredients are moistened.

2. Knead dough 4 or 5 times. Roll dough to ½-inch thickness on a lightly floured surface; cut into 6 rounds with a 2½-inch biscuit cutter.

3. Place rounds on a baking sheet coated with cooking spray. Bake at 425° for 8 to 10 minutes or until biscuits are lightly browned.

4. Meanwhile, drain pineapple, reserving juice. Combine juice, brown sugar, and cornstarch in a saucepan; stir well. Add pineapple, mixing well. Bring to a boil; reduce heat, and simmer, stirring constantly, 4 minutes or until thickened.

5. Split biscuits in half horizontally while still warm; place bottom halves on individual serving plates. Spoon pineapple mixture evenly over bottom halves. Add top biscuit halves. Top each serving with 1 tablespoon whipped topping; sprinkle evenly with toasted coconut. Yield: 6 servings.

Fruit-Filled
Chocolate Shortcakes (photo, page 59)

PREP: 15 minutes   **COOK:** 5 minutes   **FREEZE:** 5 minutes

¼ cup reduced-fat semisweet chocolate morsels
3 tablespoons chocolate syrup
1 (4½-ounce) package dessert shells (4 shells per package)
1 cup sliced fresh strawberries
1 cup sliced fresh kiwifruit (about 3 kiwifruit)
3 tablespoons apple jelly, melted
2 tablespoons nonfat sour cream

Exchanges

1½ Starch

1 Fruit

1 Fat

POINTS

5

Per Serving

254 Calories

52.6g Carbohydrate

4.9g Fat (3.6g saturated)

2.7g Fiber

3.9g Protein

33mg Cholesterol

185mg Sodium

?1mg Calcium

0.7mg Iron

1. Place chocolate morsels and syrup in a small heavy saucepan. Place over very low heat until morsels melt and mixture is smooth, stirring constantly.

2. Place dessert shells on a baking sheet lined with wax paper. Spoon chocolate mixture evenly into dessert shells. Freeze 5 minutes.

3. Combine fruit and apple jelly, stirring gently. Spoon ½ cup fruit mixture into center of each dessert shell. Dollop with sour cream. Serve immediately. Yield: 4 servings.

The chocolate hardens slightly when it's placed in the freezer five minutes, giving the shortcakes a candy coating. If you don't have time to freeze the dessert, don't worry—it's just as delicious served immediately.

Double-Chocolate Banana Pudding

PREP: 15 minutes

Exchanges

2 Starch

½ Fat

POINTS

4

Per Serving

175 Calories

32.7g Carbohydrate

3.4g Fat (1.6g saturated)

0.7g Fiber

4.3g Protein

1mg Cholesterol

244mg Sodium

85mg Calcium

0.2mg Iron

2   (3.4-ounce) packages white chocolate fat-free instant pudding mix
3½   cups fat-free milk
1   (8-ounce) carton nonfat sour cream
1   teaspoon vanilla extract
2   cups frozen reduced-calorie whipped topping, thawed
62   reduced-fat chocolate wafer cookies
3   large bananas

1. Combine first 4 ingredients in a large bowl; beat at low speed of an electric mixer 3 minutes or until thickened. Fold in whipped topping.

2. Line bottom of a 3-quart bowl with chocolate wafer cookies. Slice 1 banana, and layer slices over wafers. Spoon one-third of pudding mixture over banana. Repeat layers twice.

3. Place remaining chocolate wafers around top edge of dessert. Serve immediately; or cover and chill until ready to serve. Yield: 14 servings.

Creamy Mocha-Almond Mousse

PREP: 13 minutes   CHILL: 5 minutes

1   (8-ounce) carton coffee low-fat yogurt (or vanilla low-fat yogurt)
1½   cups fat-free milk
½   teaspoon almond extract
1   (3.4-ounce) package chocolate fat-free instant pudding mix
1¼   cups plus 2 tablespoons frozen reduced-calorie whipped topping,
        thawed and divided
2   tablespoons sliced almonds, toasted

1. Spoon yogurt onto several layers of heavy-duty paper towels;
spread to ½-inch thickness. Let stand 5 minutes. Scrape yogurt from
paper towels, using a rubber spatula; set aside.

2. Pour milk into a large bowl; add almond extract and pudding mix.
Beat with a wire whisk 1 minute. Cover and chill 5 minutes; stir in
drained yogurt. Fold 1 cup whipped topping into yogurt mixture.

3. Spoon mousse evenly into six 4-ounce parfait glasses or dessert
dishes. Top each serving with 1 tablespoon remaining whipped topping
and 1 teaspoon almonds. Serve immediately; or cover and chill until
ready to serve. Yield: 6 servings.

Exchanges
1½ Starch
½ Fat

POINTS
4

Per Serving
165 Calories
29.4g Carbohydrate
3.3g Fat (2.4g saturated)
0.2g Fiber
4.5g Protein
4mg Cholesterol
303mg Sodium
160mg Calcium
0.2mg Iron

Draining the yogurt on paper towels makes this dessert thicker and creamier. You'd never guess the mousse is low in fat.

Hummingbird Loaf Cake

PREP: 16 minutes   COOK: 5 minutes

Exchanges
1½ Starch
1 Fruit
1 Fat

POINTS
5

Per Serving
257 Calories
49.3g Carbohydrate
4.9g Fat (2.1g saturated)
0.5g Fiber
4.0g Protein
10mg Cholesterol
222mg Sodium
8mg Calcium
0.1mg Iron

¼ cup chopped pecans
½ (8-ounce) package Neufchâtel cheese (do not soften)
2 teaspoons light butter (do not soften)
2 cups sifted powdered sugar
¼ teaspoon vanilla extract
1 (8-ounce) can crushed pineapple in juice, drained
½ medium banana, chopped
1 (13.6-ounce) loaf fat-free pound cake

1. Spread pecans in a shallow pan. Bake at 350° for 5 minutes, stirring occasionally; set aside.

2. Beat Neufchâtel cheese and butter at high speed of an electric mixer until creamy. Gradually add sugar, beating well. Add vanilla, and beat until combined.

3. Combine 3 tablespoons Neufchâtel cheese mixture, pineapple, and banana; set aside. Combine remaining Neufchâtel cheese mixture and pecans, stirring well; set aside.

4. Slice cake in thirds horizontally. Place bottom cake layer on a serving plate; spread with half of pineapple mixture. Repeat layers once.

5. Place remaining cake layer on pineapple mixture. Frost top and sides of cake with reserved pecan mixture. Serve immediately; or cover and chill until ready to serve. Yield: 10 servings (1 slice per serving).

This is **speed-scratch baking** at its best. Start with a low-fat convenience product, and add a few simple ingredients. In minutes, you'll have a company-worthy dessert.

Caramel-Apple Cake (photo, page 58)

PREP: 7 minutes   COOK: 27 minutes

1   (12.5-ounce) package apple-cinnamon fat-free snack cake mix
1   cup water
2   egg whites
3   tablespoons low-fat sour cream
2½ tablespoons fat-free caramel topping
3   tablespoons chopped pecans, toasted

1. Prepare cake according to package directions, using 1 cup water and egg whites. Pour batter into an 8-inch square pan. Bake at 375° for 27 minutes or until lightly browned.

2. Meanwhile, combine sour cream and caramel topping, stirring until frosting is smooth.

3. Spread frosting over warm cake, and sprinkle with toasted pecans. Serve warm. Yield: 9 servings (1 square per serving).

To toast pecans, place pecans in a hot small nonstick skillet (no oil needed) over medium heat; cook, stirring constantly, for just 2 to 3 minutes. You'll be amazed how toasting enhances the rich flavor of the nuts.

Exchanges

1½ Starch
1 Fruit
½ Fat

POINTS

4

Per Serving

200 Calories
40.6g Carbohydrate
2.3g Fat (0.5g saturated)
0.2g Fiber
2.0g Protein
2mg Cholesterol
245mg Sodium
15mg Calcium
0.1mg Iron

Easy Chocolate Pudding Cake

PREP: 5 minutes   COOK: 30 minutes   STAND: 5 minutes

Exchanges

2 Starch

½ Fat

POINTS

4

Per Serving

182 Calories

35.8g Carbohydrate

3.1g Fat (1.7g saturated)

1.6g Fiber

2.7g Protein

0mg Cholesterol

265mg Sodium

46mg Calcium

0.6mg Iron

The sweet potatoes replace most of the fat in this moist and rich chocolate dessert.

1   (10.1-ounce) package reduced-fat devil's food cake mix

½   cup plus 2 tablespoons fat-free milk

2   tablespoons nonfat sour cream

1   teaspoon vanilla extract

1   (4-ounce) jar sweet potato baby food

Vegetable cooking spray

¼   cup firmly packed brown sugar

2   tablespoons unsweetened cocoa

1¼ cups boiling water

½   cup plus 1 tablespoon frozen reduced-calorie whipped topping, thawed

1. Combine first 5 ingredients, stirring well. Spoon batter into an 8-inch glass baking dish coated with cooking spray.

2. Combine brown sugar and cocoa; sprinkle over batter. Pour boiling water over batter (do not stir).

3. Bake at 350° for 30 minutes. Remove from oven, and let stand 5 minutes. Spoon cake into individual serving bowls; top each serving with 1 tablespoon whipped topping. Yield: 9 servings.

Fudgy-Mint Brownie Bites

PREP: 12 minutes   COOK: 16 minutes

1   (20.5-ounce) package low-fat fudge brownie mix
½   cup water
⅓   cup reduced-fat semisweet chocolate morsels
½   teaspoon peppermint extract
Vegetable cooking spray

Exchange
1 Starch

POINTS
2

Per Serving
89 Calories
16.4g Carbohydrate
2.1g Fat (0.9g saturated)
0.6g Fiber
1.2g Protein
0mg Cholesterol
72mg Sodium
0mg Calcium
0.0mg Iron

1. Combine brownie mix and water in a large bowl, stirring well. Stir in chocolate morsels and peppermint extract.

2. Spoon 1 tablespoon batter into each of 30 miniature muffin cups heavily coated with cooking spray. Bake at 350° for 16 minutes. Cool completely in pans. Yield: 2½ dozen (1 per serving).

To make pan brownies, prepare batter as directed above; spoon into a 13- x 9- x 2-inch pan heavily coated with cooking spray. Bake at 350° for 25 to 27 minutes. Place on wire rack, and cool completely. Yield: 2½ dozen.

Baked Cherry-Chocolate Turnovers

PREP: 18 minutes   COOK: 10 minutes

Exchanges
1 Starch
1 Fruit
1 Fat

POINTS
4

Per Serving
170 Calories
30.4g Carbohydrate
5.2g Fat (2.1g saturated)
0.4g Fiber
2.2g Protein
0mg Cholesterol
283mg Sodium
0mg Calcium
0.2mg Iron

¾   cup reduced-calorie cherry pie filling
1½ tablespoons no-sugar-added strawberry spread
2   tablespoons plus 1 teaspoon reduced-fat semisweet
         chocolate morsels
2   tablespoons all-purpose flour
1   (10-ounce) can refrigerated cinnamon-sugar biscuits
Vegetable cooking spray
2   tablespoons sifted powdered sugar

1. Combine first 3 ingredients; set aside.

2. Sprinkle flour evenly over work surface. Separate biscuits into rounds, and place rounds on floured surface. Roll each round to a 4½-inch circle.

3. Spoon 1½ tablespoons cherry mixture over half of each circle. Brush edges of circles with water; fold in half. Seal edges of turnovers by pressing with a fork.

4. Place turnovers on a baking sheet coated with cooking spray. Bake at 400° for 10 to 11 minutes or until lightly browned. Sprinkle with powdered sugar. Serve warm. Yield: 8 servings (1 turnover per serving).

Gingersnap-Date Balls

PREP: 15 minutes

38   reduced-fat gingersnap cookies

¼   cup chopped dates

¼   cup chopped pecans

3   tablespoons frozen orange juice concentrate, thawed and
      undiluted

2   tablespoons honey

¼   cup sifted powdered sugar

Exchange
1 Fruit

POINTS
1

Per Serving
68 Calories
12.4g Carbohydrate
2.0g Fat (0.4g saturated)
0.3g Fiber
0.5g Protein
0mg Cholesterol
41mg Sodium
2mg Calcium
0.1mg Iron

1. Position knife blade in food processor bowl; add cookies. Pulse 15 times or until cookies are finely ground. Add dates and pecans; pulse 12 times or until finely chopped. Add orange juice concentrate and honey; pulse 8 times or until mixture is evenly moistened.

2. Shape mixture into 1-inch balls. Roll balls in powdered sugar. Store in an airtight container in refrigerator. Yield: 2 dozen (1 per serving).

You can use a **plastic bag and a rolling pin** instead of the food processor to crush the cookies. Place cookies in a large heavy-duty, zip-top plastic bag. Remove air from bag, and seal securely. Finely crush cookies, using a rolling pin or meat mallet. Finely chop dates and pecans; place in a bowl. Add cookie crumbs, orange juice concentrate, and honey, stirring until dry ingredients are evenly moistened. Continue with directions in step 2.

Piña Colada Milk Shakes

PREP: 5 minutes

Exchanges

1½ Starch

1 Fruit

½ Fat

POINTS

5

Per Serving

218 Calories

47.0g Carbohydrate

2.0g Fat (1.3g saturated)

0.0g Fiber

5.0g Protein

0mg Cholesterol

88mg Sodium

33mg Calcium

0.3mg Iron

2½ cups vanilla nonfat ice cream

1 (6-ounce) can unsweetened pineapple juice

½ cup light coconut milk

¼ teaspoon rum extract

1. Place all ingredients in container of an electric blender. Cover and process until smooth, stopping once to scrape down sides. Pour evenly into three glasses; serve immediately. Yield: 3 cups (1 cup per serving).

Strawberry-Piña Colada Milk Shakes: Add 1 cup frozen unsweetened strawberries to above ingredients; cover and process until smooth. Yield: 4 cups (1 cup per serving).
Exchanges: 1½ Starch, 1 Fruit; Points: 4; Calories: 177

fish
&
shellfish

Catfish Nuggets with Tartar Sauce (photo, opposite page)

PREP: 15 minutes   COOK: 12 minutes

Exchanges
3 Lean Meat

POINTS
4

Per Serving
166 Calories
9.3g Carbohydrate
6.2g Fat (1.3g saturated)
0.3g Fiber
17.2g Protein
49mg Cholesterol
395mg Sodium
51mg Calcium
1.3mg Iron

1   egg white
2   teaspoons water
½   cup fine, dry breadcrumbs
¼   teaspoon ground red pepper
12   ounces farm-raised catfish, cut into 2-inch pieces
Butter-flavored vegetable cooking spray
2   teaspoons margarine, melted
¼   cup nonfat mayonnaise
2   teaspoons sweet pickle relish
2   teaspoons fresh lemon juice
1   teaspoon Dijon mustard
Lemon wedges (optional)

1. Combine egg white and water in a small bowl; beat well with a wire whisk. Combine breadcrumbs and pepper in a shallow dish. Dip fish pieces into egg white mixture, letting excess drip off. Roll fish pieces in breadcrumb mixture to coat.

2. Place fish pieces on a baking sheet coated with cooking spray. Coat fish with cooking spray. Drizzle evenly with margarine.

3. Bake at 450° for 12 to 14 minutes or until fish flakes easily when tested with a fork.

4. Meanwhile, combine mayonnaise and next 3 ingredients; stir mixture well. Serve fish with tarter sauce and, if desired, lemon wedges. Yield: 4 servings.

**Catfish Nuggets
with Tartar Sauce**
(recipe, opposite page)

**Hoisin-Grilled
Shrimp Kabobs**
(recipe, page 70)

Caramel-Apple Cake
(recipe, page 49)

Pineapple-Coconut Shortcake
(recipe, page 44)

Fruit-Filled Chocolate Shortcake
(recipe, page 45)

Linguine with Red Clam Sauce
(recipe, page 69)

Herb-Crusted Grouper

PREP: 13 minutes   COOK: 10 minutes

4   (4-ounce) grouper fillets
¼   teaspoon seasoned salt (or regular salt)
¼   teaspoon pepper
Butter-flavored vegetable cooking spray
3   tablespoons chopped fresh basil
3   tablespoons chopped fresh thyme
2   tablespoons chopped fresh parsley
2   teaspoons margarine
Lemon or lime wedges (optional)

1. Sprinkle fish on both sides with salt and pepper; coat with cooking spray. Spread herbs on a sheet of wax paper; roll fish in herbs to coat.

2. Melt margarine in a large nonstick skillet over medium heat. Place fish in skillet; cook 5 minutes on each side or until fish flakes easily when tested with a fork. Serve with lemon or lime wedges, if desired. Yield: 4 servings.

Exchanges
3 Very Lean Meat

POINTS
3

Per Serving
126 Calories
0.8g Carbohydrate
3.3g Fat (0.7g saturated)
0.4g Fiber
22.2g Protein
42mg Cholesterol
207mg Sodium
45mg Calcium
1.5mg Iron

Substitute dried herbs for fresh, if desired; 1 tablespoon dried equals 3 tablespoons fresh.

Cajun Grouper

PREP: 4 minutes   COOK: 18 minutes

Exchanges
3 Very Lean Meat
½ Starch

POINTS
3

Per Serving
149 Calories
6.1g Carbohydrate
3.7g Fat (0.8g saturated)
1.6g Fiber
22.9g Protein
42mg Cholesterol
478mg Sodium
135mg Calcium
7.4mg Iron

2   teaspoons margarine
1   small sweet onion, thinly sliced
1   teaspoon paprika
¾   teaspoon garlic salt
½   teaspoon dried thyme
⅛   teaspoon ground red pepper
⅛   teaspoon black pepper
4   (4-ounce) grouper fillets (or red snapper or halibut)
Olive oil-flavored vegetable cooking spray

1. Place margarine in a large ovenproof nonstick skillet over medium-high heat until hot. Add onion, and sauté 6 minutes or until tender.

2. Combine paprika and next 4 ingredients; sprinkle evenly over fish. Coat fish with cooking spray. Place fish over onion in skillet.

3. Bake at 425° for 12 minutes or until fish flakes easily when tested with a fork. Place fish and onion evenly on individual serving plates, using a slotted spoon. Yield: 4 servings.

This grouper gets its **Cajun flavor** from paprika, thyme, and red and black pepper. For a hotter, spicier kick, double the red pepper.

Halibut Provençal

PREP: 10 minutes   COOK: 10 minutes

1   cup chopped plum tomato (about 4 plum tomatoes)
2   tablespoons pitted, coarsely chopped kalamata olives (or sliced
          ripe olives)
2   tablespoons chopped fresh basil (or parsley)
1   clove garlic, minced
¼   teaspoon seasoned salt (or regular salt)
¼   teaspoon pepper
4   (4-ounce) halibut steaks
Olive oil-flavored vegetable cooking spray

1. Combine first 4 ingredients; set aside.

2. Sprinkle salt and pepper over both sides of fish; coat with cooking spray. Arrange fish in a grill basket coated with cooking spray.

3. Place on grill over medium-hot coals (350° to 400°); grill, covered, 5 to 6 minutes on each side or until fish flakes easily when tested with a fork. Top fish with tomato mixture. Yield: 4 servings.

Exchanges

3 Very Lean Meat
½ Vegetable

POINTS

3

Per Serving

145 Calories
3.0g Carbohydrate
3.7g Fat (0.5g saturated)
0.9g Fiber
24.2g Protein
36mg Cholesterol
251mg Sodium
65mg Calcium
1.4mg Iron

To **pit a kalamata olive** quickly, press the olive with the side of a chef's knife.

Grilled Glazed Salmon

PREP: 3 minutes   STAND: 10 minutes   COOK: 12 minutes

Exchanges

3 Lean Meat

½ Starch

POINTS

5

Per Serving

230 Calories

9.1g Carbohydrate

10.2g Fat (1.7g saturated)

0.1g Fiber

24.3g Protein

77mg Cholesterol

317mg Sodium

7mg Calcium

0.6mg Iron

4   (4-ounce) salmon fillets

½   teaspoon paprika

¼   teaspoon salt

2   tablespoons honey

1   tablespoon Dijon mustard

Vegetable cooking spray

1. Sprinkle fish with paprika and salt. Combine honey and mustard; brush over fish. Let stand 10 minutes.

2. Meanwhile, coat grill rack with cooking spray; place on grill over medium-hot coals (350° to 400°). Place fish on rack; grill, covered, 6 to 7 minutes on each side or until fish flakes easily when tested with a fork. Yield: 4 servings.

Salmon is a high-fat fish. Fortunately, it contains the "good" fat, **omega-3 polyunsaturated fat,** so it's particularly beneficial to heart health.

Snapper with Garlic-Cilantro Sauce

PREP: 7 minutes   COOK: 12 minutes

½   cup dry white wine
4   (4-ounce) red snapper fillets (or grouper)
½   teaspoon paprika
½   teaspoon salt
½   teaspoon finely grated lemon rind
1   clove garlic
1   cup fresh cilantro
Lemon wedges (optional)

Exchanges
3 Very Lean Meat

POINTS
3

Per Serving
140 Calories
1.6g Carbohydrate
1.7g Fat (0.3g saturated)
0.7g Fiber
23.8g Protein
42mg Cholesterol
375mg Sodium
62mg Calcium
1.4mg Iron

1. Bring wine to a simmer over medium-high heat in a large nonstick skillet. Add fish to skillet; sprinkle evenly with paprika, salt, and lemon rind. Cover, reduce heat, and simmer 8 to 10 minutes or until fish flakes easily when tested with a fork.

2. Meanwhile, position knife blade in food processor bowl. Drop garlic through food chute with processor running; process until garlic is minced. Add cilantro; process until finely chopped.

3. Transfer fish to a serving platter, using a large slotted spoon; cover with aluminum foil, and keep warm. Cook skillet juices over medium-high heat until reduced to ⅓ cup. Add cilantro mixture to skillet; cook, stirring constantly, 1 minute. Spoon sauce evenly over fish; serve with lemon wedges, if desired. Yield: 4 servings.

> One cup of **fresh cilantro** may sound like a lot, but when combined with garlic and lemon, the result is a wonderful light, citrusy sauce.

Garlic-Baked Snapper

PREP: 11 minutes   COOK: 15 minutes

Exchanges
3 Very Lean Meat
½ Starch

POINTS
3

Per Serving
140 Calories
4.7g Carbohydrate
2.0g Fat (0.4g saturated)
0.3g Fiber
24.1g Protein
42mg Cholesterol
114mg Sodium
47mg Calcium
0.6mg Iron

4   (4-ounce) red snapper fillets
Vegetable cooking spray
1   tablespoon dry sherry
¾   cup soft breadcrumbs
2   tablespoons chopped fresh parsley
½   teaspoon paprika
¼   teaspoon ground red pepper
1   or 2 cloves garlic, minced
Lemon wedges (optional)

1. Place fish in an 11- x 7- x 1½-inch baking dish coated with cooking spray; drizzle with sherry.

2. Combine breadcrumbs and next 4 ingredients; sprinkle evenly over fish. Bake, uncovered, at 400° for 15 to 20 minutes or until fish flakes easily when tested with a fork. Serve with lemon wedges, if desired. Yield: 4 servings.

To test fish for doneness, flake it with a fork at its thickest point. Properly cooked fish flakes easily and appears opaque with milky white juices.

Chipotle-Chutney Tuna Steaks

PREP: 6 minutes   **COOK:** 9 minutes

¼   cup mango chutney
1   to 2 teaspoons minced canned chipotle chiles in adobo sauce (or
       2 teaspoons fresh lime juice plus ¼ teaspoon ground red
       pepper)
4   (4-ounce) tuna steaks
Vegetable cooking spray
2   tablespoons chopped fresh cilantro

1. Combine chutney and chiles in a small bowl. Place fish on rack of
a broiler pan coated with cooking spray; spread half of chutney mixture evenly over fish.

2. Broil fish 5½ inches from heat (with electric oven door partially
opened) 5 minutes. Turn fish over; brush with remaining chutney
mixture. Broil 4 to 5 additional minutes or until fish flakes easily
when tested with a fork.

3. Place fish on individual serving plates; sprinkle cilantro evenly
over fish. Yield: 4 servings.

Grill these tuna steaks instead of broiling, if you prefer.
Coat grill rack with cooking spray; place on grill over medium
hot coals (350° to 400°). Place fish on rack; grill, covered, 4
minutes on each side.

Exchanges

3 Lean Meat
½ Starch

POINTS

5

Per Serving

209 Calories
11.1g Carbohydrate
5.7g Fat (1.4g saturated)
0.4g Fiber
26.7g Protein
43mg Cholesterol
127mg Sodium
7mg Calcium
1.6mg Iron

Asian Tuna Steaks

PREP: 3 minutes   MARINATE: 10 minutes   COOK: 9 minutes

Exchanges
3 Lean Meat

POINTS
5

Per Serving
202 Calories
1.7g Carbohydrate
8.0g Fat (1.8g saturated)
0.1g Fiber
27.3g Protein
43mg Cholesterol
529mg Sodium
4mg Calcium
1.5mg Iron

¼   cup reduced-sodium soy sauce
2   tablespoons dry sherry
2   teaspoons dark sesame oil (or vegetable oil)
1   teaspoon peeled, minced gingerroot
½   teaspoon dried crushed red pepper
½   teaspoon minced garlic
4   (4-ounce) tuna steaks
Vegetable cooking spray

1. Combine first 6 ingredients in a large heavy-duty, zip-top plastic bag. Add fish. Seal bag, and shake gently until fish is well coated. Marinate in refrigerator 10 minutes. Remove fish from marinade, reserving marinade.

2. Coat grill rack with cooking spray; place on grill over medium-hot coals (350° to 400°). Place fish on rack; grill, covered, 4 minutes on each side or until fish flakes easily when tested with a fork.

3. Place marinade in a small saucepan. Bring to a boil; reduce heat, and simmer, uncovered, 1 minute. Drizzle marinade evenly over fish. Yield: 4 servings.

Freshly grated gingerroot tastes hot, while ground ginger gives a sweet but peppery flavor—so don't try substituting one for the other. If you don't have gingerroot, increase the red pepper to ¾ teaspoon.

Linguine with Red Clam Sauce (photo, page 60)

PREP: 4 minutes   COOK: 18 minutes

8   ounces linguine, uncooked
Vegetable cooking spray
3   cloves garlic, minced
2   (14½-ounce) cans no-salt-added stewed tomatoes, undrained
¼   teaspoon dried crushed red pepper
3   (6½-ounce) cans clams, drained
⅓   cup grated Parmesan or Romano cheese

1. Cook pasta according to package directions, omitting salt and fat.

2. Meanwhile, coat a large deep skillet with cooking spray, and place over medium heat. Add garlic; cook, stirring constantly, 2 minutes. Add tomatoes and crushed red pepper to skillet. Bring mixture to a boil; reduce heat, and simmer, uncovered, 7 to 8 minutes.

3. Stir in clams; cook until thoroughly heated.

4. Drain pasta; arrange on four serving plates. Top evenly with clam sauce, and sprinkle with cheese. Yield: 4 servings.

Exchanges
2 Very Lean Meat
3 Starch
1 Vegetable
½ Fat

POINTS
7

Per Serving
371 Calories
57.1g Carbohydrate
4.1g Fat (1.5g saturated)
2.2g Fiber
25.6g Protein
41mg Cholesterol
216mg Sodium
203mg Calcium
18.2mg Iron

Hoisin-Grilled Shrimp Kabobs (photo, page 57)

PREP: 15 minutes   COOK: 8 minutes

Exchanges

3 Very Lean Meat

½ Starch

1 Fruit

POINTS

4

Per Serving

199 Calories

27.6g Carbohydrate

1.6g Fat (0.3g saturated)

1.1g Fiber

17.7g Protein

129mg Cholesterol

923mg Sodium

52mg Calcium

2.6mg Iron

1½ pounds unpeeled large fresh shrimp

1   (8-ounce) can pineapple chunks in juice, drained

1   sweet red pepper, cut into 1-inch pieces

¼   cup plus 2 tablespoons hoisin sauce

1½ teaspoons minced garlic (or 1 small clove garlic, minced)

1. Peel shrimp; devein, if desired. Drain pineapple, reserving 2 tablespoons juice.

2. Thread shrimp, pineapple chunks, and pepper pieces onto eight 10-inch metal skewers. Combine reserved pineapple juice, hoisin sauce, and garlic; stir well. Brush half of mixture over both sides of kabobs.

3. Grill kabobs, covered, over medium-hot coals (350° to 400°) 8 minutes or until shrimp turn pink, turning once and brushing with remaining hoisin sauce mixture. Yield: 4 servings.

Find **hoisin sauce** in the Asian section of the supermarket. Or make your own: Just mix 3 tablespoons brown sugar, 3 tablespoons reduced-sodium soy sauce, and ¼ teaspoon garlic powder.

meatless
main
dishes

Spinach Frittata (photo, page 78)

PREP: 7 minutes   **COOK:** 13 minutes   **STAND:** 5 minutes

Exchanges
2 Lean Meat
1 Vegetable

POINTS
3

Per Serving
154 Calories
6.9g Carbohydrate
5.1g Fat (2.3g saturated)
3.7g Fiber
15.9g Protein
10mg Cholesterol
580mg Sodium
223mg Calcium
3.5mg Iron

2   teaspoons margarine
½   cup chopped onion
1   clove garlic, minced
1½   cups egg substitute
¼   teaspoon salt
¼   teaspoon pepper
⅛   teaspoon nutmeg
1   (10-ounce) package frozen chopped spinach, thawed and drained
½   cup (2 ounces) shredded Swiss cheese
1   cup fat-free marinara sauce, warmed

1. Melt margarine in a 10-inch nonstick skillet with sloped sides over medium-high heat. Add onion and garlic; sauté until tender.

2. Combine egg substitute and next 4 ingredients; add onion mixture, stirring well. Pour egg mixture into skillet. Cover; cook over medium-low heat 10 minutes or until mixture is set. Remove from heat; sprinkle with cheese. Cover; let stand 5 minutes or until cheese melts. Serve with warm marinara sauce. Yield: 4 servings.

Thaw spinach quickly by heating it in the microwave at LOW (30% power) for 5 minutes. Break apart with a fork, and continue defrosting until thawed. Drain on paper towels to remove excess moisture.

Mexican-Style Poached Eggs (photo, page 3)

PREP: 3 minutes   COOK: 15 minutes

1   (16-ounce) can red beans, rinsed and drained
1   (14½-ounce) can Mexican-style stewed tomatoes, undrained
2   tablespoons sliced green onions
4   eggs
4   (6-inch) corn tortillas
Vegetable cooking spray
¼   teaspoon garlic powder
¼   teaspoon ground cumin
¼   cup no-salt-added salsa
¼   cup nonfat sour cream
Chopped fresh cilantro (optional)

Exchanges
1 Medium-Fat Meat
2 Starch
1 Vegetable

POINTS
5

Per Serving
293 Calories
40.8g Carbohydrate
7.0g Fat (1.8g saturated)
5.1g Fiber
17.7g Protein
221mg Cholesterol
417mg Sodium
140mg Calcium
4.3mg Iron

1. Combine first 3 ingredients in a saucepan; cook, uncovered, over medium heat 10 minutes, stirring occasionally.

2. Meanwhile, poach eggs by pouring water to depth of 2 inches into a large skillet. Bring water to a boil; reduce heat, and simmer. Break 1 egg into a saucer; slip egg into simmering water, holding saucer as close as possible to water. Repeat with remaining 3 eggs. Simmer eggs 5 minutes or until done; remove from water with a slotted spoon. Drain.

3. Coat tortillas on both sides with cooking spray. Combine garlic powder and cumin; sprinkle on 1 side of tortillas. Stack tortillas; cut stack into quarters. Place tortilla wedges in a single layer on a baking sheet; bake at 475° for 5 minutes or until crisp and golden, turning once.

4. Arrange tortilla wedges around edges of four individual serving plates; top evenly with bean mixture. Top each serving with a poached egg. Spoon 1 tablespoon salsa and 1 tablespoon sour cream over each serving. Sprinkle with cilantro, if desired. Yield: 4 servings.

If you prefer, use no-oil **baked tortilla chips** in this recipe instead of making your own chips.

Vegetable-Bean Enchiladas (photo, page 78)

PREP: 10 minutes   COOK: 15 minutes   STAND: 5 minutes

Exchanges
1 Lean Meat
1½ Starch
1 Vegetable

POINTS
4

Per Serving
226 Calories
29.7g Carbohydrate
3.8g Fat (1.6g saturated)
3.1g Fiber
10.6g Protein
9mg Cholesterol
721mg Sodium
140mg Calcium
0.9mg Iron

4   ounces sliced fresh zucchini (about 1 medium zucchini)
4   ounces sliced fresh yellow squash (about 1 medium-size yellow squash)
½   cup no-salt-added salsa, divided
¼   cup chopped fresh cilantro
1   teaspoon ground cumin
1   (16-ounce) can fat-free refried beans
8   (8-inch) fat-free flour tortillas
Vegetable cooking spray
1   (10-ounce) can enchilada sauce
1   cup (4 ounces) shredded reduced-fat Cheddar cheese
¼   cup chopped fresh cilantro

1. Combine vegetables, ¼ cup salsa, ¼ cup cilantro, and cumin in a microwave-safe bowl. Cover with heavy-duty plastic wrap, and vent. Microwave at HIGH 3 minutes. Stir; microwave 2 minutes or until vegetables are crisp-tender. Add refried beans; stir well.

2. Spoon bean mixture down centers of tortillas. Roll up; place, seam sides down, in a 13- x 9- x 2-inch baking dish coated with cooking spray. Combine remaining ¼ cup salsa and enchilada sauce; spoon over enchiladas. Cover with wax paper; microwave at HIGH 6 minutes. Rotate dish; microwave 4 to 5 minutes or until hot.

3. Uncover and sprinkle with cheese. Let stand, uncovered, 5 minutes. Sprinkle with ¼ cup cilantro. Yield: 8 servings (1 enchilada per serving).

Corn and Bean Wraps

PREP: 10 minutes   COOK: 11 minutes

Vegetable cooking spray
1   (16-ounce) package shredded coleslaw mix
1½   cups frozen whole-kernel corn
1   cup chopped green onions (about 8 green onions)
1   tablespoon salt-free Creole seasoning blend
½   teaspoon salt
1   (16-ounce) can red beans, rinsed and drained
⅓   cup nonfat mayonnaise
6   (8-inch) fat-free flour tortillas, warmed

1. Coat a large deep nonstick skillet with cooking spray; place over medium heat until hot. Add coleslaw mix; cover and cook 3 minutes. Stir well, and cook 2 additional minutes or until cabbage is wilted. Uncover; stir in corn and green onions. Sprinkle Creole seasoning and salt over slaw mixture; cook, stirring constantly, 3 minutes. Add beans; cook 2 minutes, stirring often.

2. Remove bean mixture from heat; stir in mayonnaise. Spoon evenly down centers of tortillas; fold edges of tortillas over filling, and roll up. Yield: 6 servings (1 wrap per serving).

To warm tortillas, place wax paper between tortillas; microwave at HIGH 1 minute. Or wrap tortillas in aluminum foil and bake at 350° for 10 to 12 minutes.

Exchanges
2½ Starch
2 Vegetable

POINTS
4

Per Serving
265 Calories
56.9g Carbohydrate
0.7g Fat (0.1g saturated)
5.4g Fiber
10.1g Protein
0mg Cholesterol
910mg Sodium
37mg Calcium
2.3mg Iron

Twenty-Minute Chili (photo, cover and opposite page)

PREP: 10 minutes   COOK: 10 minutes

Exchanges
2 Starch
2 Vegetable
½ Fat

POINTS
4

Per Serving
290 Calories
48.9g Carbohydrate
3.9g Fat (1.4g saturated)
11.1g Fiber
16.7g Protein
5mg Cholesterol
908mg Sodium
139mg Calcium
4.2mg Iron

1   (16-ounce) can chili hot beans, undrained
1   (15-ounce) can black beans, rinsed and drained
1   (14½-ounce) can Mexican-style stewed tomatoes, undrained
1   cup frozen whole-kernel corn
½   cup chunky salsa
1   tablespoon ground cumin
2   teaspoons chili powder
1   green pepper or sweet red pepper, coarsely chopped (about 1 cup)
¼   cup nonfat sour cream
¼   cup (1 ounce) shredded reduced-fat Cheddar cheese

1. Combine first 8 ingredients in a large saucepan; cover. Bring to a boil. Reduce heat; simmer 10 minutes, stirring occasionally. Ladle chili into individual bowls; top each serving with 1 tablespoon sour cream and 1 tablespoon cheese. Yield: 4 servings (1½ cups per serving).

This **hearty chili** is one of the easiest—and tastiest—around. Hot beans, salsa, and chili powder provide the heat, while tomatoes, peppers, and corn add garden-fresh appeal. For even more heat, add a small amount of chopped fresh pepper such as habanero, jalapeño, banana, serrano, or Scotch bonnet.

Spinach Frittata
(recipe, page 72)

Vegetable-Bean Enchilada
(recipe, page 74)

Couscous-Stuffed Tomatoes
(recipe, page 83)

79

Creamy Polenta
with Roasted Vegetables (photo, opposite page)

PREP: 12 minutes   COOK: 18 minutes

½   pound fresh asparagus spears
2   medium zucchini, cut into ¼-inch slices (about 2½ cups)
1   small purple onion, cut into ¾-inch pieces (about 1½ cups)
Vegetable cooking spray
1   teaspoon olive oil
1   teaspoon minced garlic
½   teaspoon salt, divided
1¾ cups fat-free milk
½   cup yellow cornmeal
1½ tablespoons red wine vinegar
½   teaspoon sugar
2   tablespoons freshly grated Parmesan cheese
Freshly ground pepper (optional)

Exchanges

2 Starch

2 Vegetable

1 Fat

POINTS

4

Per Serving

221 Calories

34.1g Carbohydrate

5.0g Fat (1.8g saturated)

4.3g Fiber

12.3g Protein

8mg Cholesterol

603mg Sodium

304mg Calcium

1.7mg Iron

1. Snap off and discard tough ends of asparagus; cut asparagus into 1-inch pieces. Combine asparagus, zucchini, and onion in a 15- x 10- x 1-inch jellyroll pan coated with cooking spray. Drizzle with oil; sprinkle with garlic and ¼ teaspoon salt. Stir gently until vegetables are coated. Bake at 475° for 18 minutes or until vegetables are crisp-tender and begin to brown, stirring once.

2. Meanwhile, pour milk into a medium saucepan; place over medium heat. Gradually stir in cornmeal and remaining ¼ teaspoon salt. Cook over medium heat, stirring constantly, 5 minutes or until very thick.

3. Immediately spoon cornmeal mixture into three individual serving bowls. Combine vinegar and sugar; sprinkle over vegetables. Toss well; spoon vegetables evenly over cornmeal mixture. Sprinkle evenly with cheese; sprinkle with pepper, if desired. Yield: 3 servings.

Polenta, a dish similar to thick grits in consistency, is made from cornmeal or barley. It's creamy, rich, and loaded with carbohydrates.

Tuscan-Style Peppers

PREP: 11 minutes   COOK: 13 minutes

Exchanges
½ Medium-Fat Meat
2 Starch
2 Vegetable

POINTS
4

Per Serving
244 Calories
39.5g Carbohydrate
4.3g Fat (1.7g saturated)
5.5g Fiber
13.0g Protein
8mg Cholesterol
550mg Sodium
160mg Calcium
2.6mg Iron

4   medium-size green peppers
½   cup water
1   teaspoon olive oil
3   cloves garlic, minced
1   (15.8-ounce) can Great Northern beans, rinsed and drained
1   (14-ounce) can stewed tomatoes, drained
2   teaspoons chopped fresh rosemary
1½ cups fat-free garlic-flavored croutons
½   cup (2 ounces) shredded part-skim mozzarella cheese

1. Cut off tops of green peppers; remove and discard seeds and membranes. Place peppers in an 8-inch square baking dish, and add water. Cover with heavy-duty plastic wrap, and vent. Microwave at HIGH 6 minutes. Remove from baking dish; place, cut sides down, on several layers of paper towels to drain. Set aside.

2. Meanwhile, heat oil in a large nonstick skillet over medium heat. Add garlic, and sauté 1 minute. Add beans, tomatoes, and rosemary; simmer, uncovered, 5 minutes. Stir in croutons.

3. Stuff peppers with bean mixture; return to baking dish. Top with cheese; microwave, uncovered, at HIGH 2 minutes. Yield: 4 servings.

Couscous-Stuffed Tomatoes (photo, page 79)

PREP: 13 minutes   COOK: 6 minutes

1   (6-ounce) package tomato and lentil couscous
1   cup frozen English peas, thawed
4   medium tomatoes
1   cup (4 ounces) shredded part-skim mozzarella cheese

1. Cook couscous according to package directions, omitting fat. Stir peas into cooked couscous.

2. Cut tomatoes in half; scoop out and discard pulp. Arrange tomato halves on a baking sheet. Fill tomato halves evenly with couscous mixture, and sprinkle evenly with cheese. Broil 5½ inches from heat (with electric oven door partially opened) 3 minutes or until lightly browned. Yield: 4 servings.

Exchanges

1 Lean Meat

2 Starch

2 Vegetable

POINTS

5

Per Serving

269 Calories

42.0g Carbohydrate

5.3g Fat (2.9g saturated)

3.9g Fiber

15.7g Protein

16mg Cholesterol

633mg Sodium

202mg Calcium

1.3mg Iron

Thaw frozen peas quickly in a colander placed under cold running water.

Curried Vegetable Couscous

PREP: 4 minutes   COOK: 11 minutes

Exchanges

2 Starch

2 Vegetable

1 Fruit

POINTS

5

Per Serving

293 Calories

58.6g Carbohydrate

1.6g Fat (0.2g saturated)

5.2g Fiber

13.2g Protein

0mg Cholesterol

364mg Sodium

35mg Calcium

2.5mg Iron

1 (14½-ounce) can vegetable broth, divided

⅓ cup raisins

1 cup couscous, uncooked

½ (16-ounce) package assorted fresh stir-fry vegetables

¼ cup water

2 teaspoons curry powder

¼ teaspoon ground red pepper

1 (15.8-ounce) can black-eyed peas, rinsed and drained

1. Combine 1¼ cups broth and raisins in a small saucepan. Bring to a boil, and stir in couscous. Cover, remove from heat, and let stand 5 minutes.

2. Meanwhile, combine remaining broth, stir-fry vegetables, and remaining 4 ingredients in a saucepan; stir well. Cover and simmer 7 minutes or until vegetables are crisp-tender. Serve over couscous mixture. Yield: 4 servings.

Couscous, made from wheat, fluffs up like rice when it's cooked. The best part is that it takes only five minutes to prepare. Find couscous in the rice and pasta section of your supermarket.

Brown Rice with Vegetable Sauté

PREP: 10 minutes   COOK: 15 minutes

1   cup quick-cooking brown rice
1¼   cups vegetable broth
2   teaspoons margarine
1   cup chopped onion (about 1 medium onion)
2   cups small broccoli flowerets
1   (8-ounce) package sliced fresh mushrooms
1   teaspoon dried thyme
½   teaspoon salt
½   teaspoon minced garlic
¼   teaspoon pepper
½   cup (2 ounces) shredded part-skim mozzarella cheese
3   tablespoons chopped walnuts, toasted

Exchanges

½ Lean Meat
1½ Starch
1 Vegetable
1 Fat

POINTS

4

Per Serving

216 Calories
27.5g Carbohydrate
8.9g Fat (2.1g saturated)
3.7g Fiber
10.0g Protein
8mg Cholesterol
619mg Sodium
136mg Calcium
1.9mg Iron

1. Cook rice according to package directions, using vegetable broth instead of water and omitting salt and fat.

2. Meanwhile, melt margarine in a large nonstick skillet over medium-high heat. Add onion, and cook, stirring constantly, 5 minutes. Add broccoli; cover and cook over low heat 3 minutes. Uncover; add mushrooms and next 4 ingredients. Cook, stirring constantly, 5 minutes or until mushrooms are tender.

3. Spoon ½ cup rice onto each serving plate; top each serving with ¾ cup vegetable mixture. Sprinkle evenly with cheese and walnuts. Yield: 4 servings.

Asian Vegetable Stir-Fry

PREP: 10 minutes   COOK: 18 minutes

Exchanges

2½ Starch

1 Vegetable

½ Fat

POINTS

6

Per Serving

312 Calories

57.9g Carbohydrate

2.2g Fat (0.2g saturated)

3.1g Fiber

10.6g Protein

0mg Cholesterol

589mg Sodium

99mg Calcium

2.1mg Iron

¼   cup plus 1 tablespoon low-sodium soy sauce, divided
1   (10.5-ounce) package firm tofu, drained and cut into 1-inch cubes
1   tablespoon water
1   tablespoon cornstarch
1   tablespoon rice vinegar
1   teaspoon dark sesame oil
2   cloves garlic, minced
2   teaspoons peeled, minced gingerroot
4½ cups cut assorted fresh stir-fry vegetables
4   cups hot cooked rice

1. Sprinkle 1 tablespoon soy sauce over tofu; set aside.

2. Combine water and cornstarch in a small bowl; stir until smooth. Add remaining ¼ cup soy sauce and vinegar.

3. Heat oil in a large nonstick skillet over medium-high heat. Add garlic and gingerroot; sauté 30 seconds. Add cut fresh vegetables; stir-fry 3 minutes. Stir cornstarch mixture; add to skillet. Stir-fry 3 minutes or until vegetables are crisp-tender and sauce is thickened. Add tofu mixture; cook until thoroughly heated. Serve over rice. Yield: 4 servings.

Find 16-ounce bags of cut **assorted fresh vegetables** in the produce section of your local supermarket.

Broccoli-Cheddar Potatoes

PREP: 15 minutes   COOK: 15 minutes

4   (10-ounce) baking potatoes
2   teaspoons margarine
½   cup chopped onion
1½   cups broccoli flowerets
1   medium-size yellow squash, sliced
1   tablespoon all-purpose flour
1   cup evaporated skimmed milk
½   teaspoon dried thyme
¼   teaspoon salt
¼   teaspoon pepper
1   cup (4 ounces) shredded reduced-fat Cheddar cheese, divided

1. Place potatoes on a paper towel in microwave oven. Microwave at HIGH 8 minutes. Rotate potatoes a half-turn; microwave 7 minutes or until tender. Let stand 5 minutes.

2. Meanwhile, melt margarine in a large nonstick skillet over medium heat. Add onion; cook 3 minutes, stirring often. Add broccoli and squash; cook 3 minutes, stirring often. Sprinkle flour over vegetables; stir well, and cook 30 seconds. Add milk and next 3 ingredients; stir well. Bring to a boil; reduce heat, and simmer 3 minutes or until sauce is thickened. Remove from heat; stir in ½ cup cheese.

3. Cut a lengthwise slit in top of each potato. Press ends of each potato toward center, pushing pulp up. Top evenly with vegetable mixture; sprinkle evenly with remaining ½ cup cheese. Yield: 4 servings.

Exchanges
1 Medium-Fat Meat
3 Starch
2 Vegetable

POINTS
8

Per Serving
415 Calories
68.1g Carbohydrate
7.9g Fat (3.7g saturated)
6.1g Fiber
19.9g Protein
21mg Cholesterol
479mg Sodium
464mg Calcium
4.0mg Iron

Add reduced-fat cheese at the end of cooking to maintain a creamy texture.

Roasted Vegetable Pizza

PREP: 9 minutes   COOK: 20 minutes

Exchanges

1½ Very Lean Meat

1 Starch

2 Vegetable

½ Fat

POINTS

5

Per Serving

228 Calories

31.2g Carbohydrate

4.2g Fat (1.2g saturated)

1.9g Fiber

17.5g Protein

6mg Cholesterol

606mg Sodium

108mg Calcium

0.9mg Iron

1   cup frozen whole-kernel corn

¾   cup diagonally sliced green onions (about 6 green onions)

¾   cup sliced fresh mushrooms

1   medium-size green pepper, coarsely chopped

Vegetable cooking spray

2   tablespoons grated Parmesan cheese

½   teaspoon garlic powder

1   (10-inch) thin crust Italian bread shell (such as Boboli)

1   cup roasted garlic and onion marinara sauce (such as Classico)

1½   cups (6 ounces) shredded nonfat pizza blend cheese, divided

1. Place first 4 ingredients in a 15- x 10- x 1-inch jellyroll pan coated with cooking spray; coat vegetables with cooking spray. Bake at 500° for 10 minutes, stirring halfway through cooking time.

2. Meanwhile, sprinkle Parmesan cheese and garlic powder over bread shell; spread marinara sauce over bread shell, leaving a ½-inch border. Sprinkle ¾ cup cheese over sauce. Arrange vegetables over cheese. Sprinkle with remaining ¾ cup cheese.

3. Bake at 350° on bottom rack of oven for 10 minutes or until crust is crisp and cheese is melted. Yield: 6 servings.

We found that a **jellyroll pan** works well for roasting vegetables. If the vegetables aren't in a single layer and directly exposed to heat, they won't brown.

meats

Beef and Bean Tostadas (photo, page 97)

PREP: 10 minutes   COOK: 13 minutes

Exchanges

1½ Medium-Fat Meat

1½ Starch

1 Vegetable

POINTS

5

Per Serving

267 Calories

29.2g Carbohydrate

6.8g Fat (2.8g saturated)

6.1g Fiber

22.9g Protein

42mg Cholesterol

494mg Sodium

209mg Calcium

3.1mg Iron

4	(6-inch) corn tortillas
	Vegetable cooking spray
½	pound ground round
1	cup chopped onion (about 1 medium onion)
1	tablespoon chili powder
⅓	cup salsa
1	cup canned fat-free refried beans with green chiles
½	cup (2 ounces) shredded reduced-fat sharp Cheddar cheese
1	cup shredded romaine lettuce
1	cup seeded, chopped tomato (about 1 medium tomato)

1. Coat tortillas on both sides with cooking spray; place tortillas on a large baking sheet. Bake at 475° for 5 minutes or until crisp and lightly browned, turning once. Place tortillas on four individual serving plates.

2. Meanwhile, cook ground round and onion in a large nonstick skillet over medium heat until browned, stirring until meat crumbles. Add chili powder and salsa, stirring to combine. Reduce heat, and simmer, uncovered, 3 minutes, stirring often.

3. Place beans in a small microwave-safe bowl. Cover and microwave at HIGH 45 seconds or until thoroughly heated.

4. Spread beans evenly over tortillas. Spoon meat mixture evenly over beans; top with cheese, lettuce, and tomato. Serve tostadas immediately. Yield: 4 servings.

To remove excess fat from cooked ground round, pat the meat dry with a paper towel. Wipe drippings from skillet, if necessary.

Barbecue Burritos

PREP: 10 minutes   COOK: 10 minutes

½ pound ground round
¼ cup chopped onion
½ cup no-salt-added whole-kernel corn
¼ cup barbecue sauce
2 cups thinly sliced cabbage
2 tablespoons low-fat mayonnaise
⅛ teaspoon pepper
3 (8-inch) fat-free flour tortillas
¼ cup (1 ounce) shredded reduced-fat Cheddar cheese

1. Cook ground round and onion in a large nonstick skillet over medium heat until meat is browned, stirring until it crumbles.

2. Add corn and barbecue sauce to skillet. Cook over medium heat until thoroughly heated, stirring occasionally.

3. Meanwhile, combine cabbage, mayonnaise, and pepper, stirring mixture well.

4. Place tortillas on three individual serving plates. Top evenly with beef mixture, cabbage mixture, and cheese; roll up. Yield: 3 servings.

Exchanges

2 Lean Meat
2 Starch
1 Vegetable

POINTS

6

Per Serving

310 Calories
37.1g Carbohydrate
6.9g Fat (2.5g saturated)
2.9g Fiber
24.0g Protein
50mg Cholesterol
622mg Sodium
120mg Calcium
3.1mg Iron

Find finely **shredded cabbage,** also called angel hair, at your local supermarket.

Barbecue Chopped Steaks

PREP: 9 minutes   COOK: 10 minutes

Exchanges
3 Lean Meat
½ Starch

POINTS
5

Per Serving
199 Calories
5.4g Carbohydrate
7.4g Fat (2.6g saturated)
0.3g Fiber
26.0g Protein
70mg Cholesterol
423mg Sodium
13mg Calcium
2.6mg Iron

1   pound ground round
¼   cup barbecue sauce, divided
2   tablespoons Italian-seasoned breadcrumbs
2   tablespoons minced onion
¼   teaspoon freshly ground pepper
1   egg white, lightly beaten
Vegetable cooking spray

1. Combine ground round, 2 tablespoons barbecue sauce, and next 4 ingredients, stirring well. Shape into 4 (¾-inch-thick) oval patties.

2. Coat grill rack with cooking spray; place on grill over medium-hot coals (350° to 400°). Place patties on rack; grill, covered, 5 minutes. Turn patties, and brush with remaining 2 tablespoons barbecue sauce. Grill, covered, 5 additional minutes. Yield: 4 servings.

Speedy Shepherd's Pie (photo, page 98)

PREP: 8 minutes   COOK: 15 minutes   STAND: 5 minutes

½   (22-ounce) package frozen mashed potatoes (about 3 cups)
1⅓ cups fat-free milk
1   pound ground round
1   cup fresh or frozen chopped onion
1   cup frozen peas and carrots
½   teaspoon pepper
1   (12-ounce) jar fat-free beef gravy
½   cup (2 ounces) shredded reduced-fat Cheddar cheese

1. Combine potatoes and milk in a microwave-safe bowl. Microwave at HIGH, uncovered, 8 minutes, stirring once; set aside.

2. Meanwhile, cook ground round and onion in a 10-inch ovenproof skillet over medium heat until meat is browned, stirring until meat crumbles. Add peas and carrots, pepper, and gravy. Cook over medium heat 3 minutes or until thoroughly heated, stirring often; remove mixture from heat.

3. Spoon potatoes evenly over meat mixture, leaving a 1-inch border around edge of skillet. Broil 5½ inches from heat (with electric oven door partially opened) 3 minutes or until bubbly. Sprinkle with cheese; let stand 5 minutes. Yield: 6 servings.

To ovenproof a skillet with a plastic handle, wrap the handle with heavy-duty aluminum foil before putting it in the oven.

Exchanges

2 Lean Meat
1 Starch
1 Vegetable

POINTS

5

Per Serving

236 Calories
21.8g Carbohydrate
6.9g Fat (2.2g saturated)
1.7g Fiber
23.4g Protein
50mg Cholesterol
603mg Sodium
142mg Calcium
1.8mg Iron

Steak au Poivre (photo, page 98)

PREP: 4 minutes   COOK: 18 minutes

Exchanges
3 Lean Meat

POINTS
4

Per Serving
170 Calories
1.1g Carbohydrate
5.8g Fat (2.1g saturated)
0.3g Fiber
24.3g Protein
69mg Cholesterol
215mg Sodium
14mg Calcium
3.5mg Iron

1   pound lean boneless top sirloin steak
2   teaspoons cracked black pepper
½   teaspoon garlic powder
¼   teaspoon salt
Vegetable cooking spray
¼   cup canned no-salt-added beef broth
¼   cup dry red wine
Fresh rosemary sprigs (optional)

1. Trim fat from steak. Combine pepper, garlic powder, and salt; rub over both sides of steak.

2. Coat a large nonstick skillet with cooking spray; place skillet over medium heat until hot. Add steak, and cook 7 minutes on each side or to desired degree of doneness. Transfer to a serving platter; set aside, and keep warm.

3. Add broth and wine to skillet; cook over medium heat 4 minutes or until reduced by half, stirring occasionally. Cut steak diagonally across grain into thin slices; drizzle with broth mixture. Garnish with fresh rosemary, if desired. Yield: 4 servings.

Poivre (**PWAHV-r**) is the French word for pepper. This simple recipe for steak, enhanced by cracked pepper and garlic powder, is irresistible when served *au jus*.

Gingered Beef Stir-Fry

PREP: 10 minutes   COOK: 18 minutes

¾   pound lean boneless top sirloin steak
Vegetable cooking spray
1   teaspoon vegetable oil
1   tablespoon peeled, finely grated gingerroot (or 1 tablespoon
        bottled minced ginger)
2   cloves garlic, minced (or 1½ teaspoons bottled minced garlic)
1   (16-ounce) package assorted fresh stir-fry vegetables
½   cup no-salt-added beef broth
⅓   cup reduced-sodium soy sauce
1   tablespoon cornstarch
3   cups hot cooked rice
½   cup chopped green onions (about 4 green onions)
¼   cup chopped unsalted peanuts

1. Trim fat from steak. Cut steak diagonally across grain into thin slices.

2. Coat a wok or large nonstick skillet with cooking spray; drizzle oil around top of wok, coating sides. Heat at medium-high (375°) until hot. Add steak, gingerroot, and garlic; stir-fry 3 minutes or until steak is browned. Transfer mixture to a bowl; set aside, and keep warm.

3. Add vegetables and broth to wok; bring to a boil. Cover, reduce heat, and simmer 3 minutes or until vegetables are crisp-tender.

4. Combine soy sauce and cornstarch, stirring until smooth; add to vegetable mixture. Stir in beef mixture; stir-fry 2 minutes or until sauce is thickened.

5. To serve, place ¾ cup rice on each of four individual serving plates. Top each serving with 1 cup beef mixture. Sprinkle evenly with green onions and peanuts. Yield: 4 servings.

Exchanges
3½ Lean Meat
2 Starch
1 Vegetable

POINTS
9

Per Serving
427 Calories
52.0g Carbohydrate
10.7g Fat (2.5g saturated)
4.6g Fiber
27.0g Protein
52mg Cholesterol
636mg Sodium
43mg Calcium
4.1mg Iron

Find the 16-ounce package of assorted stir-fry vegetables including snow peas, broccoli, and carrots next to bags of shredded lettuce at your local supermarket.

Savory Steaks
with Mushroom Sauce

PREP: 4 minutes   COOK: 18 minutes

Exchanges

3 Lean Meat

1 Vegetable

POINTS

5

Per Serving

211 Calories

6.0g Carbohydrate

8.1g Fat (3.0g saturated)

1.3g Fiber

25.2g Protein

70mg Cholesterol

214mg Sodium

27mg Calcium

4.5mg Iron

Make a **non-alcoholic version** of this recipe by substituting no-salt-added beef broth or water for the red wine.

4	(4-ounce) beef tenderloin steaks (about 1 inch thick)
½	teaspoon freshly ground pepper
	Vegetable cooking spray
1	tablespoon Dijon mustard
1	tablespoon Worcestershire sauce
½	cup minced onion
1	(8-ounce) package sliced fresh mushrooms
1	teaspoon dried thyme
1	teaspoon minced garlic
¼	cup dry red wine

1. Sprinkle steaks with pepper. Coat a large nonstick skillet with cooking spray; place over medium-high heat until hot. Add steaks; cook 2 minutes on each side. Reduce heat to medium; cook 3 additional minutes, turning once.

2. Remove steaks from skillet; spread mustard over steaks, and top with Worcestershire sauce. Set aside, and keep warm.

3. Coat skillet with cooking spray; add onion, and cook, stirring constantly, 2 minutes. Add mushrooms and remaining 3 ingredients; cook, stirring constantly, 5 minutes.

4. Return steaks to skillet. Cook 4 to 5 minutes or to desired degree of doneness. Transfer steaks to four individual serving plates; spoon mushroom mixture over steaks. Yield: 4 servings.

Beef and Bean Tostada
(recipe, page 90)

Speedy Shepherd's Pie
(recipe, page 93)

Steak au Poivre
(recipe, page 94)

**Rosemary-Grilled
Veal Chops**
(recipe, page 107)

**Ham and
Barley Skillet**
(recipe, page 105)

Peppered Pork with Corn Relish (photo, opposite page)

PREP: 5 minutes   COOK: 12 minutes

Vegetable cooking spray
4   (4-ounce) lean boneless pork loin chops (about ½ inch thick)
2   tablespoons jalapeño pepper jelly, divided
1½   cups frozen whole-kernel corn, thawed
½   cup diced sweet red pepper
⅓   cup chopped green onions (about 3 green onions)

1. Coat a large nonstick skillet with cooking spray, and place over medium heat until hot. Add pork; top evenly with 1 tablespoon jelly. Cook pork 3 minutes on each side. Remove pork from skillet, and keep warm.

2. Add remaining 1 tablespoon jelly to skillet; cook over low heat, stirring constantly, until melted. Add corn, red pepper, and green onions; cook over medium-high heat, stirring constantly, 2 minutes. Add pork; cook 3 minutes or until pork is done. Yield: 4 servings.

> **When chopping** green onions and pepper, chop extra; then store in the freezer in plastic zip-top freezer bags.

Exchanges
3 Lean Meat
1 Starch
1 Vegetable

POINTS
6

Per Serving
268 Calories
20.8g Carbohydrate
8.8g Fat (2.9g saturated)
2.0g Fiber
27.1g Protein
71mg Cholesterol
82mg Sodium
13mg Calcium
1.5mg Iron

Spicy-Sweet Pork Chops

PREP: 6 minutes   COOK: 10 minutes

Exchanges

3 Lean Meat

POINTS

4

Per Serving

189 Calories

1.6g Carbohydrate

8.3g Fat (2.8g saturated)

0.1g Fiber

25.1g Protein

71mg Cholesterol

224mg Sodium

15mg Calcium

1.1mg Iron

½   teaspoon ground cumin

½   teaspoon ground coriander

¼   teaspoon salt

¼   teaspoon ground allspice

¼   teaspoon ground red pepper

4   (4-ounce) lean boneless pork loin chops (about ½ inch thick)

Vegetable cooking spray

2   tablespoons low-sugar orange marmalade

2   tablespoons unsweetened orange juice

1. Combine first 5 ingredients; rub over both sides of pork.

2. Coat a large nonstick skillet with cooking spray, and place over medium-high heat until hot. Add pork; cook 3 minutes on each side. Add marmalade and juice; simmer, uncovered, 4 minutes or until pork is browned and sauce is thickened, turning once. Yield: 4 servings.

A **spice rub** is simply a blend of spices rubbed onto uncooked food to season it. The longer you leave the rub on before cooking, the more flavor you'll get.

Pork Medaillons
with Glazed Onions

PREP: 14 minutes   COOK: 16 minutes

1   pound pork tenderloin
½   teaspoon dried thyme
¼   teaspoon salt
¼   teaspoon pepper
Vegetable cooking spray
1   teaspoon olive oil
1   small purple onion, thinly sliced and separated into rings
3   tablespoons balsamic vinegar
2   teaspoons honey

1. Trim fat from pork. Cut pork into 1-inch-thick slices. Place slices between two sheets of heavy-duty plastic wrap, and flatten to ½-inch thickness, using a meat mallet or rolling pin. Sprinkle with thyme, salt, and pepper.

2. Place a large nonstick skillet coated with cooking spray over medium heat until hot. Add pork; cook 3 minutes on each side or until browned. Remove from skillet, and keep warm.

3. Heat oil in skillet over medium heat; add onion. Cook 8 to 10 minutes or until onion is tender, stirring often. Add vinegar and honey; cook, stirring constantly, 1 minute or until onion is glazed. Spoon onion over pork. Yield: 4 servings.

Exchanges
3 Very Lean Meat
2 Vegetable
½ Fat

POINTS
4

Per Serving
182 Calories
10.6g Carbohydrate
4.5g Fat (1.3g saturated)
1.9g Fiber
24.8g Protein
74mg Cholesterol
207mg Sodium
113mg Calcium
7.9mg Iron

Ask your butcher to trim the fat from the pork tenderloin and cut it into slices while you finish grocery shopping.

Szechuan Pork Stir-Fry

PREP: 21 minutes   COOK: 8 minutes

Exchanges

3 Very Lean Meat

2 Vegetable

POINTS

3

Per Serving

149 Calories

10.1g Carbohydrate

2.6g Fat (0.8g saturated)

1.8g Fiber

19.6g Protein

55mg Cholesterol

549mg Sodium

58mg Calcium

2.5mg Iron

¾   pound pork tenderloin

¼   cup plus 2 tablespoons reduced-sodium teriyaki sauce, divided

½   teaspoon dried crushed red pepper

Vegetable cooking spray

2   cups sliced bok choy

1   cup fresh snow pea pods, diagonally cut in half

1   large sweet red pepper, cut into thin strips

1   teaspoon cornstarch

1. Trim fat from pork. Cut pork into ¼-inch-thick slices. Cut each slice into 3 strips.

2. Combine 2 tablespoons teriyaki sauce and crushed red pepper in a bowl; add pork strips, and toss well.

3. Coat a wok or large nonstick skillet with cooking spray; heat at medium heat (350°) until hot. Add pork mixture; stir-fry 3 minutes or until pork is browned. Remove from wok, and keep warm.

4. Coat wok with cooking spray. Add bok choy, snow peas, and red pepper strips; stir-fry 3 minutes.

5. Combine remaining ¼ cup teriyaki sauce and cornstarch, stirring until smooth. Add to vegetable mixture; stir-fry 1 minute. Add pork mixture to vegetable mixture, and stir-fry 1 minute. Yield: 4 servings.

You can substitute boneless center-cut pork loin chops for the pork tenderloin in this recipe. Cut the pork chops into thin strips; the cook times are the same.

Ham and Barley Skillet (photo, page 99)

1   (16-ounce) can reduced-sodium chicken broth
1   cup quick-cooking barley, uncooked
1   (16-ounce) package frozen broccoli, red pepper, onion, and
      mushrooms
10 ounces reduced-fat, low-salt ham, chopped
1   teaspoon salt-free Creole seasoning blend

1. Place broth in a medium saucepan; bring to a boil. Add barley.
Cover, reduce heat, and simmer 12 minutes.

2. Meanwhile, thaw vegetables according to package directions. Stir
vegetables, ham, and Creole seasoning into barley mixture.

3. Cover and cook 5 additional minutes or until liquid is absorbed and
vegetables are tender. Yield: 4 servings.

Ten ounces ham equals about 2 cups chopped. This is a
perfect recipe to make with any leftover ham.

Exchanges
2 Lean Meat
2 Starch
1 Vegetable

POINTS
5

Per Serving
313 Calories
47.7g Carbohydrate
4.1g Fat (0.1g saturated)
10.3g Fiber
21.8g Protein
35mg Cholesterol
844mg Sodium
14mg Calcium
1.2mg Iron

Middle Eastern Lamb Chops

PREP: 10 minutes   COOK: 10 minutes   STAND: 5 minutes

Exchanges

3 Lean Meat

2 Starch

1 Vegetable

POINTS

7

Per Serving

356 Calories

34.5g Carbohydrate

9.0g Fat (3.0g saturated)

2.3g Fiber

32.9g Protein

81mg Cholesterol

468mg Sodium

24mg Calcium

2.8mg Iron

8   (3-ounce) lean lamb loin chops (1 inch thick)

1   teaspoon curry powder

¼   teaspoon salt

⅛   teaspoon ground red pepper

Vegetable cooking spray

1   (16-ounce) can reduced-sodium chicken broth

¾   cup (1½-inch-long) carrot strips (about 1 medium carrot)

1   cup couscous, uncooked

1   tablespoon chopped fresh mint (or 1 teaspoon dried mint)

1. Trim fat from lamb. Combine curry powder, salt, and red pepper; rub evenly over both sides of lamb.

2. Coat a large nonstick skillet with cooking spray. Place skillet over medium-high heat until hot. Add lamb; cook 3 to 4 minutes on each side or to desired degree of doneness. Remove lamb from skillet. Set aside; keep warm. Wipe drippings from skillet with a paper towel.

3. Add broth and carrot strips to skillet. Bring to a boil. Reduce heat, and simmer, uncovered, 3 to 4 minutes or until carrot is crisp-tender. Stir in couscous and mint. Return lamb to skillet. Cover, remove from heat, and let stand 5 minutes.

4. Transfer chops to individual serving plates; fluff couscous mixture with a fork. Serve with lamb chops. Yield: 4 servings.

Rosemary-Grilled Veal Chops (photo, page 99)

PREP: 4 minutes   COOK: 10 minutes

4   (6-ounce) lean veal loin chops (¾ inch thick)
Olive oil-flavored vegetable cooking spray
1½ teaspoons dried rosemary, crushed
¾   teaspoon lemon-pepper seasoning

1. Trim fat from veal. Coat both sides of veal with cooking spray.
Combine rosemary and lemon-pepper seasoning; rub evenly over veal.

2. Coat grill rack with cooking spray; place on grill over medium-hot
coals (350° to 400°). Place veal on rack; grill, covered, 5 to 6 minutes
on each side or until done. Yield: 4 servings.

Exchanges
3 Lean Meat

POINTS
5

Per Serving
187 Calories
0.3g Carbohydrate
10.7g Fat (4.5g saturated)
0.1g Fiber
21.1g Protein
88mg Cholesterol
140mg Sodium
21mg Calcium
0.0mg Iron

Intensify the flavor of dried herbs by crushing them between your fingers or by using a mortar and pestle.

Veal Cutlets Paprikash

PREP: 5 minutes   COOK: 15 minutes

Exchanges
3 Lean Meat
1 Vegetable

POINTS
4

Per Serving
188 Calories
6.3g Carbohydrate
6.1g Fat (1.4g saturated)
1.3g Fiber
26.1g Protein
94mg Cholesterol
411mg Sodium
28mg Calcium
2.1mg Iron

1   pound (¼-inch-thick) veal cutlets
2   teaspoons paprika, divided
½   teaspoon salt
¼   teaspoon ground red pepper
Vegetable cooking spray
2   teaspoons olive oil, divided
1   (8-ounce) package sliced fresh mushrooms
⅓   cup finely chopped onion
⅓   cup nonfat sour cream
2   tablespoons chopped fresh parsley

1. Sprinkle veal evenly with 1 teaspoon paprika, salt, and red pepper. Coat a large nonstick skillet with cooking spray; add 1 teaspoon oil, and place over medium-high heat until hot. Add half of veal; cook 2 minutes on each side or until browned. Remove veal from skillet; set aside, and keep warm. Repeat procedure with remaining 1 teaspoon oil and remaining veal.

2. Coat skillet with cooking spray. Add mushrooms and onion; cook over medium heat 5 minutes. Add sour cream and remaining 1 teaspoon paprika to mushroom mixture; cook until thoroughly heated.

3. To serve, place veal on individual serving plates; spoon mushroom mixture evenly over veal, and sprinkle with parsley. Yield: 4 servings.

Paprika, onions, and sour cream are common ingredients in the Hungarian dish paprikash. It's typically made with chicken, but here veal is used with the same traditional flavors.

poultry

Herbed Dijon Chicken Strips (photo, page 119)

PREP: 8 minutes   COOK: 20 minutes

Exchanges

3 Very Lean Meat

½ Starch

POINTS

4

Per Serving

167 Calories

5.3g Carbohydrate

2.8g Fat (0.9g saturated)

0.3g Fiber

28.1g Protein

68mg Cholesterol

234mg Sodium

68mg Calcium

1.5mg Iron

¼   cup fine, dry breadcrumbs

2   tablespoons grated Parmesan cheese

½   teaspoon dried Italian seasoning

4   (4-ounce) skinned, boned chicken breast halves

1½ teaspoons Dijon mustard

Vegetable cooking spray

1. Combine first 3 ingredients in a large heavy-duty, zip-top plastic bag; set aside.

2. Brush chicken breast halves evenly with mustard; cut each breast into 3 strips. Add chicken to breadcrumb mixture. Seal bag; shake until chicken is coated.

3. Place chicken strips on rack of a broiler pan coated with cooking spray. Bake at 400° for 20 minutes or until done. Yield: 4 servings.

Serve these **chicken strips** with any low-fat dipping sauce, such as honey mustard, sweet-and-sour sauce, or ketchup.

Sweet-and-Sour Chicken

PREP: 12 minutes   COOK: 18 minutes

1   (8-ounce) can pineapple chunks in juice, undrained
2½   cups water, divided
⅓   cup cider vinegar
¼   cup firmly packed brown sugar
1   tablespoon low-sodium soy sauce
½   teaspoon salt
Vegetable cooking spray
4   (4-ounce) skinned, boned chicken breast halves, cut
       crosswise into thin strips
2   tablespoons cornstarch
1   cup thinly sliced onion (about 1 medium onion)
1   cup thinly sliced green pepper (about 1 medium pepper)
1½   cups instant rice, uncooked

Exchanges
3 Very Lean Meat
1 Starch
1 Fruit

POINTS
5

Per Serving
246 Calories
37.5g Carbohydrate
1.2g Fat (0.3g saturated)
1.4g Fiber
19.7g Protein
44mg Cholesterol
315mg Sodium
28mg Calcium
2.1mg Iron

1. Drain pineapple, reserving juice. Set pineapple aside. Combine juice, ½ cup water, and next 4 ingredients; set aside.

2. Coat a large nonstick skillet with cooking spray; place skillet over medium-high heat until hot. Add chicken; cook, stirring constantly, until lightly browned. Add juice mixture to skillet. Bring to a boil. Reduce heat; simmer, uncovered, 10 minutes, stirring occasionally.

3. Combine cornstarch and ½ cup water; add to skillet. Cook, stirring constantly, 1 minute or until sauce is slightly thickened. Add pineapple, onion, and green pepper. Cover; simmer 5 minutes or until vegetables are crisp-tender, stirring occasionally.

4. Meanwhile, combine rice and remaining 1½ cups water in a saucepan. Bring to a boil. Cover, remove from heat, and let stand 5 minutes or until liquid is absorbed and rice is tender. Spoon ¾ cup rice onto each individual serving plate. Top evenly with chicken mixture. Yield: 6 servings.

Fiesta Chicken and Rice

PREP: 6 minutes   COOK: 24 minutes

Exchanges
2½ Very Lean Meat
1½ Starch
1 Vegetable

POINTS
4

Per Serving
229 Calories
30.8g Carbohydrate
2.0g Fat (0.4g saturated)
2.1g Fiber
20.7g Protein
44mg Cholesterol
329mg Sodium
47mg Calcium
2.4mg Iron

Chop canned whole tomatoes while the tomatoes are still in the can, using kitchen scissors.

1   (14½-ounce) can no-salt-added whole tomatoes, undrained
1   (4.5-ounce) can chopped green chiles, undrained
Vegetable cooking spray
1   teaspoon olive oil
1   cup long-grain rice, uncooked
¾   cup chopped onion (about 1 small onion)
2   cloves garlic, minced
1   pound skinned, boned chicken breasts, cut into bite-size pieces
½   teaspoon salt
¼   teaspoon pepper
¼   teaspoon ground cumin

1. Drain tomatoes and green chiles, reserving liquid from each together in a 1-cup liquid measuring cup. Add water to reserved liquid to measure 1 cup; set aside. Chop tomatoes; set tomato and chiles aside.

2. Coat a large nonstick skillet with cooking spray; add oil. Place over medium heat until hot. Add rice, onion, and garlic; sauté 3 minutes or until rice is golden.

3. Stir tomato, green chiles, reserved 1 cup liquid, chicken, and remaining ingredients into rice mixture.

4. Bring to a boil; cover, reduce heat, and simmer 20 minutes or until liquid is absorbed and rice is tender. Yield: 6 servings.

Rosemary-Grilled Chicken

PREP: 3 minutes   MARINATE: 15 minutes   COOK: 12 minutes

½   cup dry white wine
2   tablespoons lemon juice
1½ teaspoons dried rosemary, crushed
½   teaspoon pepper
¼   teaspoon salt
2   cloves garlic, minced
4   (4-ounce) skinned, boned chicken breast halves
Vegetable cooking spray

1. Combine first 7 ingredients in a large heavy-duty, zip-top plastic bag. Seal bag, and shake until chicken is well coated. Marinate chicken in refrigerator at least 15 minutes.

2. Remove chicken from marinade, discarding marinade. Coat grill rack with cooking spray, and place on grill over medium-hot coals (350° to 400°). Place chicken on rack; grill, covered, 6 minutes on each side or until done. Yield: 4 servings.

For a **30-minute meal**, begin with this easy two-step dish. While the chicken marinates, make a green salad and your favorite flavored couscous or rice.

Exchanges
3 Very Lean Meat

POINTS
4

Per Serving
169 Calories
2.0g Carbohydrate
3.3g Fat (0.9g saturated)
0.2g Fiber
26.6g Protein
72mg Cholesterol
212mg Sodium
25mg Calcium
1.2mg Iron

Saucy Lemon Chicken

PREP: 11 minutes   COOK: 19 minutes

Exchanges

3 Very Lean Meat

1 Starch

POINTS

4

Per Serving

203 Calories

12.3g Carbohydrate

4.6g Fat (1.0g saturated)

0.1g Fiber

27.0g Protein

72mg Cholesterol

292mg Sodium

24mg Calcium

1.1mg Iron

Vegetable cooking spray

4   (4-ounce) skinned, boned chicken breast halves

2   teaspoons reduced-calorie margarine

¼   cup firmly packed brown sugar

¼   cup fresh lemon juice (about 2 lemons)

1   teaspoon dry mustard

¼   teaspoon salt

¼   teaspoon pepper

4   thin lemon slices

1   tablespoon cornstarch

½   cup canned reduced-sodium chicken broth

1. Coat a large nonstick skillet with cooking spray; place skillet over medium-high heat until hot. Add chicken, and cook 3 minutes on each side or until browned. Remove chicken from skillet.

2. Melt margarine in skillet over medium-low heat; stir in brown sugar and next 4 ingredients. Return chicken to skillet; cover and cook 3 minutes. Turn chicken. Top each breast with a lemon slice; cover and cook 3 additional minutes or until chicken is done. Transfer chicken and lemon slices to a serving plate; keep warm.

3. Combine cornstarch and broth; add to mixture in skillet. Cook, stirring constantly, 1 minute or until sauce is thickened. Spoon evenly over chicken. Yield: 4 servings.

Pair this saucy dish with **quick-cooking rice** for an easy meal. Just make the rice while the chicken browns. A family-size bag of quick-cooking rice yields four cups of cooked rice and takes only 10 minutes to cook.

Greek Chicken
with Lemon Couscous (photo, page 118)

PREP: 10 minutes   COOK: 12 minutes

1	teaspoon dried oregano
½	teaspoon garlic powder
¼	teaspoon salt
¼	teaspoon pepper
4	(4-ounce) skinned, boned chicken breast halves

Vegetable cooking spray

1¼	cups canned reduced-sodium chicken broth
1	tablespoon grated lemon rind
3	tablespoons fresh lemon juice (about 2 lemons)
2	teaspoons reduced-calorie margarine
1	teaspoon dried parsley flakes
1	(10-ounce) package couscous, uncooked

Lemon slices (optional)

Fresh oregano sprigs (optional)

Exchanges

3 Very Lean Meat

2½ Starch

POINTS

8

Per Serving

401 Calories

52.1g Carbohydrate

5.0g Fat (1.0g saturated)

2.6g Fiber

36.3g Protein

72mg Cholesterol

385mg Sodium

23mg Calcium

2.5mg Iron

1. Combine first 4 ingredients; sprinkle over both sides of chicken. Place chicken on rack of a broiler pan coated with cooking spray. Broil 5½ inches from heat (with electric oven door partially opened) 12 minutes or until done, turning once.

2. Meanwhile, combine broth and next 4 ingredients in a saucepan; bring to a boil. Remove from heat, and stir in couscous. Cover and let stand 5 minutes or until liquid is absorbed and couscous is tender.

3. Spoon couscous evenly onto four serving plates; top each serving with a chicken breast half. If desired, garnish with lemon slices and oregano sprigs. Yield: 4 servings.

Chicken with Spiced Peach Sauce (photo, opposite page)

PREP: 12 minutes   COOK: 16 minutes

1   (16-ounce) can sliced peaches in light syrup, undrained

¼   cup low-sugar orange marmalade

¼   teaspoon ground nutmeg

¼   teaspoon ground ginger

¼   teaspoon salt

⅛   teaspoon pepper

Vegetable cooking spray

6   (4-ounce) skinned, boned chicken breast halves

1   teaspoon cornstarch

2   tablespoons water

1. Drain peaches, reserving ½ cup syrup. Set peaches aside. Combine ½ cup syrup, marmalade, and next 4 ingredients; set aside.

2. Coat a large nonstick skillet with cooking spray; place skillet over medium-high heat until hot. Add chicken, and cook 5 minutes or until browned on both sides, turning once. Add peaches and marmalade mixture to chicken; bring to a boil. Cover and cook 10 minutes or until chicken is done.

3. Remove chicken from skillet, and keep warm. Combine cornstarch and water; add to peach mixture. Bring to a boil; cook, stirring constantly, 1 minute or until sauce is thickened. Spoon sauce evenly over chicken. Yield: 6 servings.

Greek Chicken with Lemon Couscous
(recipe, page 115)

Herbed Dijon Chicken Strips
(recipe, page 110)

**Turkey, Peppers, and
Basil with Pasta**
(recipe, page 126)

**Old-Fashioned
Turkey Hash**
(recipe, page 128)

Chicken and Dumplings
(recipe, page 123)

Chicken with Mushroom Sauce

PREP: 10 minutes   COOK: 23 minutes

1   (16-ounce) can reduced-sodium chicken broth
2   tablespoons all-purpose flour
¼   teaspoon salt
¼   teaspoon pepper
4   (4-ounce) skinned, boned chicken breast halves
Vegetable cooking spray
1   (8-ounce) package sliced fresh mushrooms
½   cup thinly sliced green onions (about 2 green onions)
2   cloves garlic, minced
½   teaspoon ground thyme

1. Bring broth to a boil in a small saucepan; boil 5 minutes.

2. Meanwhile, combine flour, salt, and pepper in a large heavy-duty, zip-top plastic bag; add chicken. Seal bag, and shake until chicken is well coated.

3. Coat a large nonstick skillet with cooking spray; place skillet over medium heat until hot. Add chicken, and cook 2 minutes on each side or until lightly browned. Remove chicken from skillet; set aside.

4. Coat skillet with cooking spray; place over medium heat until hot. Add mushrooms and remaining 3 ingredients; cook, stirring constantly, 3 minutes.

5. Add broth and chicken to skillet; bring to a boil. Reduce heat, and simmer 12 to 15 minutes or until chicken is done. Yield: 4 servings.

Exchanges
3 Very Lean Meat
1½ Vegetable

POINTS
4

Per Serving
187 Calories
7.7g Carbohydrate
3.4g Fat (0.9g saturated)
1.2g Fiber
29.8g Protein
72mg Cholesterol
454mg Sodium
32mg Calcium
2.2mg Iron

Tropical Grilled Chicken

PREP: 8 minutes   **COOK:** 18 minutes

Exchanges

2½ Very Lean Meat

½ Starch

POINTS

3

Per Serving

134 Calories

6.3g Carbohydrate

3.9g Fat (0.9g saturated)

0.1g Fiber

16.8g Protein

71mg Cholesterol

296mg Sodium

10mg Calcium

0.9mg Iron

½   cup reduced-calorie apricot-pineapple preserves
¼   cup Dijon mustard
½   teaspoon grated orange rind
3   tablespoons fresh orange juice
½   teaspoon ground ginger
3   green onions, finely chopped
8   large skinned chicken thighs (about 3 pounds)
Vegetable cooking spray

1. Combine first 6 ingredients in a small bowl. Brush half of preserves mixture over both sides of chicken. Set remaining mixture aside.

2. Coat grill rack with cooking spray; place on grill over medium-hot coals (350° to 400°). Place chicken on rack, meaty side down; brush with half of reserved preserves mixture. Grill, covered, 9 minutes. Turn chicken, and brush with remaining preserves mixture. Grill, covered, 9 additional minutes or until chicken is done. Yield: 8 servings.

The secrets to **delicious grilled chicken** are proper temperature of the coals, correct placement of the grill rack, and the right amount of cooking time. Place the rack about six inches above medium-hot coals.

Chicken and Dumplings (photo, page 120)

PREP: 6 minutes   COOK: 24 minutes

4   (14¼-ounce) cans no-salt-added chicken broth
1   cup chopped celery (about 3 stalks celery)
1   cup chopped onion (about 1 medium onion)
1   cup chopped carrot (about 1 medium carrot)
½   teaspoon salt
¼   to ½ teaspoon pepper
2   cups reduced-fat biscuit and baking mix (such as Bisquick)
1   teaspoon dried parsley flakes
¾   cup fat-free milk
3   cups shredded commercial roasted chicken

1. Combine first 6 ingredients in a Dutch oven; bring to a boil. Cover, reduce heat to medium, and cook 5 minutes.

2. Meanwhile, combine biscuit mix and parsley flakes. Add milk, stirring with a fork just until dry ingredients are moistened.

3. Return broth mixture to a boil. Drop dough by teaspoonfuls into boiling broth; reduce heat to medium. Cover and cook 10 minutes, stirring once.

4. Add chicken to broth mixture, stirring gently. Cook, uncovered, 5 additional minutes. Yield: 6 servings.

Exchanges
2 Medium-Fat Meat
2 Starch
1 Vegetable

POINTS
7

Per Serving
330 Calories
34.4g Carbohydrate
9.2g Fat (2.1g saturated)
1.4g Fiber
24.1g Protein
54mg Cholesterol
636mg Sodium
80mg Calcium
1.3mg Iron

A Dutch oven is a wide, large, deep pot with a tight-fitting lid.

Turkey with Chutney Glaze

PREP: 7 minutes   COOK: 17 minutes

Exchanges

3 Very Lean Meat

1½ Starch

POINTS

5

Per Serving

238 Calories

28.6g Carbohydrate

1.5g Fat (0.5g saturated)

0.2g Fiber

24.1g Protein

60mg Cholesterol

692mg Sodium

16mg Calcium

1.9mg Iron

2   (½-pound) turkey tenderloins

Vegetable cooking spray

½   cup chopped mango chutney

1   tablespoon Dijon mustard

1   teaspoon curry powder

1. Place turkey on rack of a broiler pan coated with cooking spray. Combine chutney, mustard, and curry powder, stirring well. Brush turkey with half of chutney mixture.

2. Broil turkey 5½ inches from heat (with electric oven door partially opened) 9 minutes. Turn turkey, and brush with remaining chutney mixture. Broil 8 to 10 additional minutes or until done. Cut turkey diagonally across grain into thin slices. Yield: 4 servings.

Find **mango chutney** as well as many other flavored chutneys in the condiment section or bottled sauce section of the supermarket.

Santa Fe Turkey Skillet

PREP: 15 minutes   COOK: 13 minutes

2   (½-pound) turkey tenderloins, cut crosswise into ¼-inch-thick
        slices
1½ tablespoons chili powder
Vegetable cooking spray
8   green onions, cut into 1-inch pieces
1   large clove garlic, minced
1   (15-ounce) can no-salt-added black beans, rinsed and drained
1   (10-ounce) package frozen whole-kernel corn, thawed
¼   cup water
1   tablespoon fresh lime juice
¼   teaspoon salt
8   cherry tomatoes, halved

1. Combine turkey and chili powder, tossing until turkey is coated. Coat a large nonstick skillet with cooking spray; place over medium-high heat until hot. Add turkey, and sauté 5 minutes or until done. Remove turkey from skillet, set aside.

2. Coat skillet with cooking spray; place over medium-high heat until hot. Add green onions and garlic to skillet; sauté 2 minutes. Add beans and next 4 ingredients; cook, stirring constantly, 3 minutes or until mixture is thoroughly heated.

3. Add turkey and tomatoes to skillet; cook, stirring constantly, until mixture is thoroughly heated. Yield: 4 servings.

Exchanges
3 Very Lean Meat
2 Starch

POINTS
4

Per Serving
269 Calories
37.5g Carbohydrate
2.1g Fat (0.4g saturated)
9.6g Fiber
28.1g Protein
45mg Cholesterol
378mg Sodium
46mg Calcium
2.8mg Iron

Sauté means to cook food in a skillet in a small amount of oil or cooking spray over medium-high heat, stirring constantly, for a short period of time.

Turkey, Peppers, and Basil with Pasta (photo, page 119)

PREP: 15 minutes   COOK: 15 minutes

Exchanges

3 Very Lean Meat

2 Starch

2 Vegetable

POINTS

7

Per Serving

356 Calories

48.1g Carbohydrate

4.2g Fat (1.3g saturated)

1.9g Fiber

30.8g Protein

57mg Cholesterol

381mg Sodium

123mg Calcium

4.6mg Iron

8   ounces spaghetti, uncooked

Vegetable cooking spray

1   teaspoon olive oil

1   pound turkey cutlets, cut into 1-inch pieces

2   cloves garlic, minced

2   large green or sweet red peppers, cut into thin strips

2   (14½-ounce) cans no-salt-added diced tomatoes, undrained

½   teaspoon salt

½   teaspoon pepper

½   cup sliced fresh basil

3   tablespoons grated Parmesan cheese

Fresh basil sprigs (optional)

1. Cook pasta according to package directions, omitting salt and fat. Drain; set aside, and keep warm.

2. Meanwhile, coat a large nonstick skillet with cooking spray; add oil, and place over medium heat until hot. Add turkey and garlic; cook, stirring constantly, 3 minutes.

3. Add pepper strips; cook 5 minutes. Add tomato, salt, and ½ teaspoon pepper; cook over medium heat 5 minutes, stirring occasionally. Stir in sliced basil; cook until thoroughly heated.

4. Divide pasta evenly among five serving plates; top evenly with turkey mixture, and sprinkle with Parmesan cheese. Garnish with basil sprigs, if desired. Yield: 5 servings.

In general, **allow one to two ounces uncooked pasta** per person. Eight ounces dry spaghetti will yield four to five cups cooked pasta.

Turkey Picadillo

PREP: 6 minutes   COOK: 20 minutes

2¾ cups water
1¼ cups long-grain rice, uncooked
Vegetable cooking spray
1   pound freshly ground raw turkey
1   cup chopped onion (about 1 medium onion)
1   cup peeled, chopped cooking apple (about 1 medium apple)
¼   cup raisins
2   tablespoons sliced pimiento-stuffed olives
1   tablespoon canned diced jalapeño pepper
½   teaspoon salt
¼   teaspoon pepper
¼   teaspoon ground cinnamon
⅛   teaspoon ground cloves
1   (14½-ounce) can no-salt-added diced tomatoes, undrained
1   (8-ounce) can tomato sauce

1. Bring water to a boil in a medium saucepan over high heat. Add rice; stir well. Cover, reduce heat, and simmer 20 minutes or until liquid is absorbed and rice is tender.

2. Meanwhile, coat a large nonstick skillet with cooking spray; place skillet over medium heat until hot. Add turkey and onion; cook, stirring constantly, until turkey is browned and onion is tender.

3. Add apple and remaining 9 ingredients to skillet; cover and cook 15 minutes, stirring occasionally.

4. Place ⅔ cup rice on each of six individual serving plates, and top evenly with turkey mixture. Yield: 6 servings.

Exchanges
3 Very Lean Meat
1½ Starch
1 Vegetable
1 Fruit

POINTS
6

Per Serving
307 Calories
48.8g Carbohydrate
3.0g Fat (0.8g saturated)
2.9g Fiber
20.8g Protein
49mg Cholesterol
796mg Sodium
64mg Calcium
3.2mg Iron

Old-Fashioned Turkey Hash (photo, page 120)

PREP: 9 minutes   COOK: 20 minutes

Exchanges
3 Very Lean Meat
1½ Starch

POINTS
4

Per Serving
224 Calories
21.4g Carbohydrate
4.4g Fat (1.1g saturated)
4.9g Fiber
25.3g Protein
27mg Cholesterol
1054mg Sodium
94mg Calcium
1.4mg Iron

Vegetable cooking spray
1   teaspoon vegetable oil
2   cups cubed cooked turkey breast
1   cup chopped onion
1   (15-ounce) can sliced cooked potatoes, drained
⅔   cup fat-free milk
½   cup no-salt-added chicken broth
¼   teaspoon freshly ground pepper
¼   teaspoon ground thyme
4   (¾-ounce) slices light wheat sandwich bread, toasted
Freshly ground pepper

1. Coat a large nonstick skillet with cooking spray; add oil, and place over medium-high heat until hot. Add turkey, onion, and potato; cook 10 minutes or until onion is tender and potato is browned, stirring occasionally.

2. Add milk and next 3 ingredients to turkey mixture; bring to a boil. Reduce heat, and simmer, uncovered, 8 to 10 minutes or to desired consistency, stirring occasionally.

3. Cut slices of toast in half diagonally, and place on four individual serving plates. Spoon hash mixture evenly over toast. Sprinkle with freshly ground pepper. Yield: 4 servings.

Turkey Stroganoff on Sage Biscuits

PREP: 5 minutes   COOK: 15 minutes

1   cup reduced-fat biscuit and baking mix (such as Bisquick)
¾   teaspoon ground sage
¼   teaspoon pepper, divided
¼   cup plus 2 tablespoons fat-free milk
Vegetable cooking spray
¼   cup chopped onion (about ½ small onion)
1   (10¾-ounce) can 98% fat-free cream of chicken soup, undiluted
½   cup fat-free milk
2   cups cubed cooked turkey breast
½   cup low-fat sour cream
Chopped fresh parsley (optional)

Exchanges

2½ Very Lean Meat

2 Starch

1 Fat

POINTS

7

Per Serving

339 Calories

33.5g Carbohydrate

9.3g Fat (4.0g saturated)

0.5g Fiber

27.4g Protein

68mg Cholesterol

731mg Sodium

125mg Calcium

1.5mg Iron

1. Combine biscuit mix, sage, and ⅛ teaspoon pepper; add ¼ cup plus 2 tablespoons milk, stirring just until dry ingredients are moistened and mixture forms a soft dough. Drop dough in 4 equal portions onto a baking sheet coated with cooking spray. Bake at 425° for 8 to 10 minutes or until lightly browned.

2. Meanwhile, coat a large nonstick skillet with cooking spray; place over medium heat until hot. Add onion; sauté 3 minutes or until tender. Combine soup, ½ cup milk, and remaining ⅛ teaspoon pepper, stirring with a wire whisk until smooth.

3. Stir soup mixture and turkey into onion. Bring to a boil; cover, reduce heat, and simmer 3 minutes, stirring occasionally. Remove from heat; stir in sour cream. Cook over low heat, stirring constantly, just until mixture is thoroughly heated. (Do not boil.)

4. Cut each biscuit in half; place 2 halves on each of four individual serving plates. Spoon turkey mixture evenly over biscuits. Sprinkle with parsley, if desired; serve immediately. Yield: 4 servings.

For an **easy variation,** serve the turkey stroganoff mixture over whole wheat toast points instead of biscuits.

Pasta with Sausage and Vegetables

PREP: 13 minutes   COOK: 17 minutes

Exchanges

1½ Medium-Fat Meat

2 Starch

3 Vegetable

POINTS

7

Per Serving

341 Calories

50.1g Carbohydrate

6.9g Fat (2.9g saturated)

2.7g Fiber

17.4g Protein

34mg Cholesterol

1022mg Sodium

16mg Calcium

1.6mg Iron

Penne, ziti, and rotini pastas are good substitutions for rigatoni; they're similar in size and shape.

12   ounces rigatoni (tubular pasta), uncooked

Vegetable cooking spray

1   pound smoked turkey sausage, cut into ½-inch pieces

2   medium-size green peppers, cut into ½-inch pieces

1   medium onion, cut into eighths

1   clove garlic, minced

1   (26-ounce) jar fat-free chunky pasta sauce with mushrooms

1. Cook pasta according to package directions, omitting salt and fat. Drain and set aside.

2. Meanwhile, coat a Dutch oven with cooking spray; place over medium heat until hot. Add sausage; cook 5 minutes or until browned, stirring often. Remove sausage from Dutch oven; set aside. Wipe drippings from Dutch oven with a paper towel.

3. Coat Dutch oven with cooking spray; place over medium heat until hot. Add pepper, onion, and garlic; cook 5 minutes, stirring often. Add sausage and pasta sauce; bring to a boil. Reduce heat, and simmer 5 minutes, stirring occasionally. Toss pasta with sausage mixture. Serve immediately. Yield: 7 servings (1½ cups per serving).

salads

Minted Melon-Cucumber Salad (photo, page 138)

PREP: 20 minutes

Exchange
1 Fruit

POINTS
1

Per Serving
61 Calories
14.6g Carbohydrate
0.5g Fat (0.2g saturated)
1.4g Fiber
1.2g Protein
0mg Cholesterol
7mg Sodium
18mg Calcium
0.4mg Iron

2	cups cubed cantaloupe
2	cups cubed watermelon
1	cup thinly sliced cucumber (about 1 small cucumber)
2	tablespoons chopped fresh mint
2	tablespoons sugar
1	tablespoon minced onion
3	tablespoons raspberry-flavored vinegar

1. Combine first 4 ingredients in a large bowl.

2. Combine sugar, onion, and vinegar in a small jar. Cover tightly, and shake vigorously. Pour over melon mixture; toss gently.

3. Serve immediately; or cover and chill up to 2 hours. Serve with a slotted spoon. Yield: 6 servings (1 cup per serving).

Buy cubed **watermelon and cantaloupe** in the produce section of the supermarket to make this salad superquick.

Tropical Fruit Salad

PREP: 25 minutes

1¼ cups cubed ripe mango (about 1 medium mango)
1   cup chopped ripe papaya (about 1 medium papaya)
1   cup chopped fresh pineapple
2   kiwifruit, peeled, cut in half lengthwise, and sliced
1   medium banana, sliced
1   tablespoon fresh lime juice, divided
½   cup vanilla low-fat yogurt
1   tablespoon honey

1. Combine first 4 ingredients in a large bowl.

2. Toss banana with 2 teaspoons lime juice. Add banana mixture to mango mixture; toss gently.

3. Combine remaining 1 teaspoon lime juice, yogurt, and honey; stir well. Spoon fruit evenly onto individual salad plates. Drizzle yogurt mixture evenly over salads. Yield: 4 servings (1 cup per serving).

Exchanges

½ Starch

2 Fruit

POINTS

2

Per Serving

161 Calories

38.1g Carbohydrate

1.1g Fat (0.4g saturated)

4.3g Fiber

2.9g Protein

1mg Cholesterol

22mg Sodium

79mg Calcium

0.6mg Iron

For an elegant dessert, spoon the fruit into your favorite wine glasses.

Greek Spinach Salad

PREP: 15 minutes

Exchanges
½ Starch
2 Vegetable
1 Fat

POINTS
2

Per Serving
126 Calories
17.2g Carbohydrate
4.2g Fat (1.3g saturated)
3.4g Fiber
6.3g Protein
5mg Cholesterol
186mg Sodium
86mg Calcium
2.3mg Iron

¼ cup red wine vinegar
1 tablespoon water
2 teaspoons olive oil
½ teaspoon dried oregano
1 or 2 cloves garlic, minced
1 (15-ounce) can garbanzo beans, drained
1½ cups sliced cucumber (about 1 medium cucumber)
1½ cups chopped plum tomato (about 5 plum tomatoes)
5 cups loosely packed torn spinach
⅓ cup crumbled feta cheese
Freshly ground pepper (optional)

1. Combine first 5 ingredients, stirring well with a wire whisk. Combine beans, cucumber, and tomato in a large bowl; add vinegar mixture, tossing well.

2. Add spinach and feta cheese; toss salad gently. Sprinkle salad with pepper, if desired. Arrange salad evenly on individual salad plates. Yield: 6 servings (1½ cups per serving).

Try a flavored **feta cheese** like tomato-basil or black peppercorn for variety.

Mixed Greens with Bacon-Horseradish Dressing

PREP: 3 minutes   COOK: 5 minutes

6   slices turkey bacon
½   cup nonfat buttermilk
2   tablespoons nonfat mayonnaise
1   teaspoon prepared horseradish
⅛   teaspoon salt
⅛   teaspoon freshly ground pepper
6   cups torn mixed salad greens
1   cup sliced fresh mushrooms
Freshly ground pepper (optional)

1. Place bacon a on microwave-safe plate lined with paper towels. Microwave at HIGH 5 minutes. Crumble bacon.

2. Combine buttermilk and next 4 ingredients, stirring well.

3. Combine salad greens and mushrooms; arrange evenly on six salad plates. Spoon 2 tablespoons buttermilk dressing over each salad; sprinkle evenly with bacon. Sprinkle with freshly ground pepper, if desired. Yield: 6 servings.

Exchanges
1 Medium-Fat Meat
1 Vegetable

POINTS
3

Per Serving
126 Calories
3.4g Carbohydrate
7.3g Fat (1.9g saturated)
0.9g Fiber
8.7g Protein
36mg Cholesterol
844mg Sodium
42mg Calcium
0.6mg Iron

Mixed Antipasto Salad (photo, opposite page)

PREP: 15 minutes

Exchanges
2 Vegetable
½ Fat

POINTS
2

Per Serving
93 Calories
12.9g Carbohydrate
2.8g Fat (1.3g saturated)
1.5g Fiber
5.9g Protein
7mg Cholesterol
510mg Sodium
118mg Calcium
1.7mg Iron

4   cups torn romaine lettuce
1½   cups small whole fresh mushrooms, sliced
⅓   cup sliced purple onion
¼   cup sliced ripe olives
2   ounces part-skim mozzarella cheese, cut into cubes
1   (14-ounce) can artichoke hearts, drained and quartered
1   (7-ounce) jar roasted sweet red peppers, drained and
       coarsely chopped
¼   cup fat-free Italian herb and cheese dressing (such as
       Hidden Valley)
¼   teaspoon fresh coarsely ground pepper

1. Combine first 7 ingredients in a large bowl. Add dressing; toss well. Sprinkle evenly with pepper. Yield: 5 servings (1½ cups per serving).

Look for **convenient 16-ounce packages** of torn romaine lettuce in the produce section of your local supermarket.

Mixed Antipasto Salad
(recipe, opposite page)

Spicy Chicken Finger Salad
(recipe, page 144)

Minted Melon-Cucumber Salad
(recipe, page 132)

**Black Bean-
Rice Salad**
(recipe, page 141)

Chunky Asian Slaw

PREP: 14 minutes

4   cups coarsely shredded napa cabbage
1   cup fresh Sugar Snap peas, cut in half
⅓   cup thinly sliced sweet red pepper
¼   cup diagonally sliced green onions (about 2 green onions)
2   tablespoons rice vinegar
1   tablespoon hoisin sauce
½   teaspoon dark sesame oil
2   tablespoons chopped unsalted peanuts

1. Combine first 4 ingredients in a large bowl.

2. Combine vinegar, hoisin sauce, and oil, stirring well. Pour vinegar mixture over cabbage mixture; toss well.

3. Serve immediately; or cover and chill. Sprinkle with peanuts just before serving. Yield: 5 servings (1 cup per serving).

Find **hoisin sauce** in the Asian section of the supermarket. Or make your own: Just mix 3 tablespoons brown sugar, 3 tablespoons reduced-sodium soy sauce, and ¼ teaspoon garlic powder.

Exchanges
1 Vegetable
½ Fat

POINTS
1

Per Serving
53 Calories
6.6g Carbohydrate
2.4g Fat (0.3g saturated)
1.6g Fiber
2.3g Protein
0mg Cholesterol
134mg Sodium
58mg Calcium
1.1mg Iron

Creamy Mustard-Dill Potato Salad

PREP: 11 minutes   CHILL: 2 hours

Exchanges
1 Starch
½ Fat

POINTS
2

Per Serving
114 Calories
18.9g Carbohydrate
2.8g Fat (0.7g saturated)
2.0g Fiber
2.7g Protein
3mg Cholesterol
399mg Sodium
19mg Calcium
0.4mg Iron

2   (15-ounce) cans whole baby potatoes, drained and quartered
½   cup sliced celery
1   tablespoon minced onion
¼   cup reduced-fat mayonnaise
¼   cup nonfat sour cream
1   tablespoon mustard
2   teaspoons minced fresh dillweed (or ½ teaspoon dried dillweed)
⅛   teaspoon pepper

1. Combine first 3 ingredients in a large bowl.

2. Combine mayonnaise and remaining 4 ingredients, stirring well. Add mayonnaise mixture to potato mixture; toss gently until combined. Cover and chill at least 2 hours. Yield: 6 servings (½ cup per serving).

You can **substitute dried herbs** in most recipes calling for fresh ones, but use only one-third the amount—their flavor is stronger than fresh. Dried herbs and spices lose their flavor and intensity over time. To maximize the shelf life of seasonings, store them in the freezer or in a cool, dry place.

Black Bean-Rice Salad (photo, page 138)

(photo, page 138)

PREP: 5 minutes   **COOK:** 7 minutes   **CHILL:** 30 minutes

1	(16-ounce) package frozen rice pilaf with vegetables
1	(15-ounce) can black beans, rinsed and drained
3	tablespoons reduced-fat olive oil vinaigrette
1	tablespoon lemon juice
¼	teaspoon salt
¼	teaspoon hot sauce
⅛	teaspoon pepper

1. Cook pilaf according to package directions, omitting salt and fat.

2. Transfer rice pilaf to a large bowl. Add beans and remaining ingredients to rice pilaf; toss mixture well. Cover and chill 30 minutes. Yield: 4 servings (1 cup per serving).

Exchanges

2 Starch

1 Vegetable

½ Fat

POINTS

4

Per Serving

205 Calories

38.4g Carbohydrate

3.2g Fat (0.1g saturated)

4.3g Fiber

7.9g Protein

0mg Cholesterol

397mg Sodium

16mg Calcium

1.5mg Iron

Vegetarian Taco Salad

PREP: 12 minutes

Exchanges

1 Very Lean Meat

2 Starch

1 Vegetable

1 Fat

POINTS

6

Per Serving

333 Calories

51.6g Carbohydrate

7.5g Fat (2.8g saturated)

5.3g Fiber

15.4g Protein

11mg Cholesterol

627mg Sodium

143mg Calcium

3.0mg Iron

1   (16-ounce) can kidney beans, rinsed and drained

1   (8¾-ounce) can no-salt-added whole-kernel corn, drained

1   (4.5-ounce) can chopped green chiles, undrained

1   cup diced tomato (about 1 medium tomato)

½   cup low-fat sour cream

¼   cup chopped green onions (about 2 green onions)

1   tablespoon 40%-less-sodium taco seasoning

5   cups shredded mixed salad greens

½   (13.5-ounce) bag salsa- and cream cheese-flavored baked tortilla chips (about 6 cups)

½   cup (2 ounces) shredded nonfat Cheddar cheese, divided

1. Combine first 7 ingredients in a large bowl; stir well. Add salad greens, and toss gently to coat.

2. To serve, divide tortilla chips evenly among four individual serving plates. Top each serving with salad mixture, and sprinkle with 2 tablespoons cheese. Yield: 4 servings.

This taco salad is a **complete one-dish meal**—it's loaded with vegetables, beans, cheese, and tortilla chips.

Vegetable-Tortellini Salad (photo, page 4)

PREP: 15 minutes   COOK: 15 minutes

3   tablespoons balsamic vinegar
1   tablespoon pesto sauce
¼   teaspoon salt
¼   teaspoon pepper
1   clove garlic, minced
2   ears fresh corn, husks removed
1   medium zucchini, cut into ½-inch pieces
1   small purple onion, cut into 6 wedges
Vegetable cooking spray
1   (9-ounce) package refrigerated cheese-filled tortellini, uncooked
½   cup dried tomato halves (packed without oil)

1. Combine first 5 ingredients in a small bowl, stirring well.

2. Brush corn, zucchini, and onion with half of vinegar mixture, reserving remaining vinegar mixture. Coat grill rack with cooking spray. Grill vegetables, covered, over medium-hot coals (350° to 400°) 12 to 15 minutes, turning occasionally.

3. Meanwhile, cook pasta according to package directions, omitting salt and fat. Add dried tomato for last 5 minutes of cooking. Drain pasta and tomato; coarsely chop tomato.

4. Cut corn kernels from cob. Add corn kernels, zucchini, and onion to pasta mixture; pour reserved vinegar mixture over pasta mixture, and toss well. Yield: 4 servings (1¼ cups per serving).

Exchanges
1 Very Lean Meat
2½ Starch
1 Fat

POINTS
6

Per Serving
289 Calories
46.0g Carbohydrate
6.5g Fat (1.8g saturated)
2.6g Fiber
13.3g Protein
29mg Cholesterol
558mg Sodium
43mg Calcium
0.9mg Iron

To find out if **fresh ears of corn** are at their sweetest, pop open a kernel with your fingernail. If the juice is milky white, the corn is sweet.

Spicy Chicken Finger Salad (photo, page 137)

PREP: 7 minutes   COOK: 15 minutes

Exchanges
2 Lean Meat
1 Starch
1 Vegetable

POINTS
4

Per Serving
222 Calories
21.2g Carbohydrate
3.8g Fat (1.7g saturated)
2.4g Fiber
30.4g Protein
71mg Cholesterol
664mg Sodium
90mg Calcium
2.3mg Iron

This recipe was a **staff favorite.** The flavors will remind you of spicy Buffalo chicken wings.

⅓   cup cornflake crumbs
2   teaspoons chili powder
½   teaspoon garlic powder
1   pound chicken breast tenderloins
Vegetable cooking spray
6   cups torn romaine lettuce
1   cup sliced celery
½   cup sliced purple onion
½   cup commercial fat-free Ranch-style dressing
2   teaspoons hot sauce
¼   cup crumbled blue cheese

1. Combine first 3 ingredients in a heavy-duty, zip-top plastic bag; add chicken. Seal bag, and shake until chicken is well coated.

2. Place chicken on a baking sheet coated with cooking spray. Bake at 375° for 15 minutes or until chicken is done.

3. Combine lettuce, celery, and onion. Combine dressing and hot sauce; pour over lettuce mixture, and toss well.

4. Place lettuce mixture evenly on four individual serving plates. Arrange chicken evenly over salads; sprinkle each serving with 1 tablespoon cheese. Yield: 4 servings.

sides

Gingered Pears

PREP: 10 minutes   COOK: 10 minutes

2	teaspoons margarine
1	large firm ripe red pear, cut into eighths
1	large firm ripe green pear, cut into eighths
1	teaspoon grated orange rind
¼	cup unsweetened orange juice
1	tablespoon honey
2	teaspoons finely chopped crystallized ginger

1. Melt margarine in a nonstick skillet over medium heat. Add pear pieces; cook 2 to 3 minutes. Remove pear with a slotted spoon. Set aside, and keep warm.

2. Add orange rind and remaining 3 ingredients to skillet. Bring to a boil; cook 3 minutes or until mixture is reduced by half. Return pear to skillet, and cook until pear is tender. Yield: 4 servings.

Crystallized ginger is gingerroot that has been cooked in a sugar syrup and coated with coarse sugar.

Mustard Potatoes and Green Beans (photo, page 155)

PREP: 9 minutes   COOK: 16 minutes

6   small round red potatoes, quartered
1   pound fresh green beans, trimmed
2   tablespoons canned reduced-sodium chicken broth
1   tablespoon coarse-grained mustard
2   teaspoons olive oil
½   teaspoon salt
½   teaspoon dried rosemary, crushed

1. Place potatoes in a medium saucepan; add water to cover. Bring to a boil; cook 3 minutes. Add green beans; cover, reduce heat to medium, and cook 12 minutes or until potato and beans are tender. Drain.

2. Combine broth and remaining 4 ingredients. Pour over potato mixture; toss gently to coat. Yield: 5 servings (1 cup per serving).

Substitute a one-pound bag of frozen **green beans** for fresh beans, if desired. Bring potato to a boil, and cook 8 minutes. Add frozen beans; cook 7 additional minutes or until potato and beans are tender. Continue with recipe as directed.

Exchanges
1 Starch
1 Vegetable
½ Fat

POINTS
2

Per Serving
112 Calories
21.3g Carbohydrate
2.2g Fat (0.3g saturated)
3.1g Fiber
3.5g Protein
0mg Cholesterol
287mg Sodium
41mg Calcium
1.6mg Iron

Broccoli with Caraway-Cheese Sauce

PREP: 7 minutes   COOK: 12 minutes

Exchanges

1 Vegetable

½ Fat

POINTS

1

Per Serving

58 Calories

6.3g Carbohydrate

2.4g Fat (0.9g saturated)

2.3g Fiber

4.2g Protein

4mg Cholesterol

128mg Sodium

100mg Calcium

0.8mg Iron

2	pounds fresh broccoli
2	teaspoons margarine
¾	cup fat-free milk
1½	tablespoons all-purpose flour
¼	teaspoon salt
⅛	teaspoon pepper
¼	cup (1 ounce) shredded Gruyère or Swiss cheese
½	teaspoon caraway seeds
1	(2-ounce) jar diced pimiento, drained

1. Remove and discard broccoli leaves; cut off and discard tough ends of stalks. Wash broccoli; cut into spears. Arrange spears in a steamer basket over boiling water. Cover and steam 8 minutes or until crisp-tender. Drain and place on a serving platter; set aside, and keep warm.

2. Meanwhile, melt margarine in a saucepan over medium heat. Add milk and next 3 ingredients; cook, stirring constantly with a wire whisk, until smooth. Add cheese and caraway seeds; cook, stirring constantly, until cheese melts and mixture is thickened and bubbly.

3. Pour sauce over broccoli. Sprinkle with pimiento, and serve immediately. Yield: 8 servings.

Caraway seeds have a distinct nutty flavor. Store the seeds in an airtight container in a cool, dark place up to six months to maintain this flavor.

Lemon-Dill Carrots and Celery

PREP: 7 minutes   COOK: 16 minutes

4   cups diagonally sliced carrot (about 7 carrots)
2   cups water
2   cups diagonally sliced celery (about 4 stalks celery)
1½ tablespoons lemon juice
1   tablespoon margarine, melted
½   teaspoon dried dillweed
¼   teaspoon salt

1. Combine carrot and water in a large saucepan; bring to a boil. Cover, reduce heat, and simmer 10 minutes. Add celery, and cook 5 additional minutes or until carrot and celery are tender.

2. Drain carrot mixture, reserving 1 tablespoon cooking liquid. Combine liquid, lemon juice, and remaining 3 ingredients. Pour over carrot mixture; toss well. Yield: 8 servings (½ cup per serving).

Exchange
1 Vegetable

POINTS
1

Per Serving
45 Calories
7.7g Carbohydrate
1.6g Fat (0.3g saturated)
2.4g Fiber
0.9g Protein
0mg Cholesterol
134mg Sodium
29mg Calcium
0.5mg Iron

If you have **fresh dill-weed** on hand, use 2 teaspoons minced fresh in place of the dried dillweed in this recipe.

Sweet Potato Casserole

PREP: 8 minutes   COOK: 6 minutes

Exchanges
1½ Starch
1 Fat

POINTS
3

Per Serving
165 Calories
29.3g Carbohydrate
4.6g Fat (1.0g saturated)
3.4g Fiber
2.5g Protein
3mg Cholesterol
134mg Sodium
33mg Calcium
0.7mg Iron

2   (14½-ounce) cans mashed sweet potato
¼   teaspoon ground allspice
Vegetable cooking spray
3   tablespoons light process cream cheese
2   tablespoons brown sugar
1   tablespoon margarine
⅓   cup drained crushed pineapple
¼   teaspoon salt
3   tablespoons chopped pecans, toasted

1. Combine sweet potato and allspice in a mixing bowl. Beat mixture at medium speed of an electric mixer 2 minutes or until smooth. Spoon into a 1-quart microwave-safe baking dish coated with cooking spray. Cover and microwave at HIGH 5 minutes or until thoroughly heated.

2. Add cheese, sugar, and margarine to sweet potato mixture. Beat at medium speed until combined. Stir in pineapple and salt.

3. Microwave, uncovered, at HIGH 1 minute or until mixture is thoroughly heated. Sprinkle with toasted pecans, and serve warm. Yield: 8 servings (½ cup per serving).

Toast pecans to bring out a strong, rich flavor. Place pecans in a shallow dish, and microwave 2 to 4 minutes at HIGH, stopping every 30 seconds to stir.

Roasted Squash and Peppers

PREP: 5 minutes   COOK: 13 minutes

3   small yellow squash
3   small zucchini
2   medium-size sweet red peppers
Olive oil-flavored vegetable cooking spray
1   teaspoon dried oregano
¼   teaspoon salt
¼   teaspoon pepper
1   tablespoon balsamic vinegar

Exchanges

2 Vegetable

POINTS

Free

Per Serving

50 Calories
10.1g Carbohydrate
1.0g Fat (0.1g saturated)
3.0g Fiber
2.5g Protein
0mg Cholesterol
153mg Sodium
39mg Calcium
1.8mg Iron

1. Cut squash and zucchini in half crosswise. Cut halves lengthwise into ½-inch-thick wedges. Cut peppers into 2-inch-long strips. Set pepper strips aside.

2. Coat a large baking sheet with cooking spray. Place squash and zucchini in a single layer on baking sheet; coat vegetables with cooking spray. Sprinkle with oregano, salt, and pepper.

3. Bake at 500° for 5 minutes. Turn squash and zucchini gently; add pepper strips. Bake 8 additional minutes or to desired degree of doneness. Transfer vegetables to a serving bowl. Add vinegar to vegetables, and toss gently. Yield: 4 servings (1 cup per serving).

Roasting fruits and vegetables is a simple and low-fat method of cooking. It locks in flavors while caramelizing the outer layers.

Cheese-Stuffed Tomatoes

PREP: 13 minutes   COOK: 12 minutes

Exchanges
1½ Vegetable
½ Fat

POINTS
1

Per Serving
66 Calories
7.1g Carbohydrate
2.6g Fat (1.5g saturated)
1.3g Fiber
4.4g Protein
8mg Cholesterol
191mg Sodium
98mg Calcium
0.5mg Iron

This **delicious side dish** is elegant enough to serve to company.

4   small firm, ripe tomatoes
2   tablespoons fat-free balsamic vinaigrette
16   small basil leaves
2   ounces part-skim mozzarella slices, cut into 8 (2-inch) squares
1   teaspoon Italian-seasoned breadcrumbs
¼   teaspoon freshly ground pepper

1. Cut a ⅛-inch-thick slice off bottom of each tomato (so tomato will sit flat in baking dish). Remove stem portion from top of tomato.

2. Cut each tomato horizontally into thirds. Place 4 bottom tomato slices in an 11- x 7- x 1½-inch baking dish; brush evenly with 2 teaspoons vinaigrette. Top each with 2 basil leaves and a cheese slice. Repeat layers.

3. Top with remaining 4 tomato slices; brush with remaining 2 teaspoons vinaigrette. Sprinkle evenly with breadcrumbs and pepper. Bake at 350° for 12 minutes or until cheese melts. Serve tomatoes immediately. Yield: 4 servings.

Mediterranean Couscous

PREP: 8 minutes   COOK: 5 minutes

1	(5.8-ounce) package roasted garlic and olive oil couscous mix (with seasoning packet)
1	(14-ounce) can artichoke hearts, drained and chopped
1¼	cups chopped tomato (about 1 large tomato)
½	cup crumbled feta cheese
¼	cup sliced ripe olives
1	tablespoon chopped fresh parsley
2	tablespoons lemon juice
1	teaspoon dried oregano
¼	teaspoon pepper

1. Prepare couscous according to package directions, omitting fat and using 1 tablespoon seasoning from seasoning packet; discard remaining seasoning. Fluff couscous with a fork.

2. Add chopped artichoke and remaining ingredients to couscous; toss gently. Serve warm or chilled. Yield: 7 servings.

Vary the flavor slightly in this recipe by using a flavored feta cheese such as tomato-basil or black peppercorn.

Exchanges
1½ Starch
½ Fat

POINTS
3

Per Serving
144 Calories
24.1g Carbohydrate
3.5g Fat (1.6g saturated)
1.5g Fiber
6.0g Protein
9mg Cholesterol
262mg Sodium
77mg Calcium
1.1mg Iron

Garlic-Cheese Grits

PREP: 9 minutes   COOK: 7 minutes

Exchanges
½ Medium-Fat Meat
1½ Starch

POINTS
3

Per Serving
142 Calories
21.4g Carbohydrate
2.2g Fat (0.6g saturated)
1.3g Fiber
9.3g Protein
0mg Cholesterol
507mg Sodium
201mg Calcium
0.9mg Iron

Light process American cheese melts quickly and makes these grits smooth and creamy.

4   cups water
¼   teaspoon salt
2   large cloves garlic, minced
1   cup quick-cooking grits, uncooked
6   ounces light process American cheese, cubed
½   teaspoon low-sodium Worcestershire sauce
¼   teaspoon dry mustard
⅛   teaspoon ground red pepper

1. Combine first 3 ingredients in a medium saucepan; bring to a boil. Slowly stir in grits; cover, reduce heat, and simmer 5 minutes or until grits are thickened, stirring occasionally.

2. Add cheese and remaining ingredients to grits; stir until cheese melts. Serve immediately. Yield: 6 servings.

**Mustard Potatoes
and Green Beans**
(recipe, page 147)

**Parmesan Orzo
and Peas**
(recipe, page 158)

Spicy Peanut Pasta (photo, opposite page)

PREP: 5 minutes   COOK: 10 minutes

6   ounces vermicelli, uncooked
1   (16-ounce) package frozen Sugar Snap pea stir-fry mix
¼   cup reduced-fat chunky peanut butter
3   tablespoons rice wine vinegar
3   tablespoons low-sodium soy sauce
2   teaspoons sugar
2   teaspoons sesame oil
½   to 1 teaspoon sweet red pepper flakes
3   tablespoons diagonally sliced green onions (about 1 green onion)

1. Cook pasta according to package directions, omitting salt and fat. Add Sugar Snap pea mix for last 4 minutes of cooking. Drain pasta mixture, and place in a serving bowl; keep warm.

2. Meanwhile, combine peanut butter and next 5 ingredients in a small saucepan. Cook over medium heat until peanut butter melts, stirring often. Add to pasta mixture; toss well. Sprinkle with green onions. Serve immediately. Yield: 10 servings (½ cup per serving).

You'll enjoy the distinct combination of **Asian flavors**— peanut butter, soy sauce, and red pepper—in this creamy pasta side dish.

Exchanges
1½ Starch
½ Fat

POINTS
3

Per Serving
151 Calories
23.3g Carbohydrate
3.8g Fat (0.7g saturated)
2.9g Fiber
6.4g Protein
0mg Cholesterol
243mg Sodium
15mg Calcium
5.5mg Iron

Parmesan Orzo and Peas (photo, page 155)

PREP: 7 minutes   COOK: 25 minutes

Exchanges
1½ Starch
½ Fat

POINTS
3

Per Serving
146 Calories
21.8g Carbohydrate
3.1g Fat (1.1g saturated)
2.1g Fiber
6.5g Protein
4mg Cholesterol
168mg Sodium
104mg Calcium
1.1mg Iron

⅓ cup dried tomato bits (packed without oil)
¾ cup hot water
1 tablespoon margarine
1 cup chopped onion
1 teaspoon minced garlic
1 cup orzo, uncooked
1 (14½-ounce) can no-salt-added chicken broth
1¼ cups frozen English peas
½ cup grated Parmesan cheese
½ cup evaporated skimmed milk

1. Combine tomato bits and hot water in a small bowl; let stand 10 minutes. Drain and set aside.

2. Meanwhile, melt margarine in a saucepan over medium-high heat. Add onion and garlic; sauté 5 minutes or until tender. Add orzo, and sauté 3 minutes or until orzo is lightly browned. Add broth, and bring to a boil. Cover, reduce heat, and simmer 12 to 15 minutes or until broth is absorbed and orzo is tender.

3. Stir in peas, cheese, and milk; cook over medium heat until cheese melts. Stir in tomato; serve immediately. Yield: 10 servings.

Try **sun-dried tomatoes** for intense tomato flavor. You can store an unopened package in the pantry up to one year; it will keep for three months once opened.

Rice with Black-Eyed Peas

PREP: 3 minutes   COOK: 5 minutes   STAND: 5 minutes

Vegetable cooking spray
1   teaspoon vegetable oil
1½   cups frozen onion and pepper seasoning blend
1   teaspoon minced garlic
1½   cups canned reduced-sodium chicken broth
1   teaspoon dried thyme
¼   teaspoon salt
1½   cups instant rice, uncooked
1   (15.8-ounce) can black-eyed peas, drained
1   teaspoon hot sauce

1. Coat a large saucepan with cooking spray, and add oil. Place over medium-high heat until hot. Add seasoning blend and garlic; sauté 4 minutes.

2. Add broth, thyme, and salt to seasoning blend mixture. Bring to a boil. Add rice, stirring well.

3. Cover, remove from heat, and let stand 5 minutes or until liquid is absorbed and rice is tender. Stir in peas and hot sauce. Serve immediately. Yield: 8 servings (½ cup per serving).

A one-cup serving makes a satisfying **meatless main dish** with 238 calories and 5 points.

Exchanges
1½ Starch

POINTS
2

Per Serving
119 Calories
21.8g Carbohydrate
1.1g Fat (0.2g saturated)
0.9g Fiber
4.9g Protein
0mg Cholesterol
243mg Sodium
17mg Calcium
1.4mg Iron

Waldorf Pilaf

PREP: 10 minutes   COOK: 5 minutes

Exchanges
1 Starch
½ Fat

POINTS
2

Per Serving
100 Calories
16.6g Carbohydrate
3.0g Fat (0.2g saturated)
1.1g Fiber
2.7g Protein
2mg Cholesterol
163mg Sodium
11mg Calcium
0.4mg Iron

1½ cups canned reduced-sodium chicken broth
½   cup apple juice
½   cup chopped celery
¼   cup chopped onion
1   (6.2-ounce) package fast-cooking long-grain and wild rice mix
      (with seasoning packet)
¾   cup finely chopped apple
⅓   cup chopped pecans, toasted
3   tablespoons chopped fresh parsley

1. Combine first 4 ingredients and 1 tablespoon seasoning from seasoning packet in a saucepan; discard remaining seasoning.

2. Bring to a boil; add rice mix. Cover, reduce heat, and simmer 5 minutes or until liquid is absorbed and rice is tender.

3. Remove rice mixture from heat; stir in apple, pecans, and parsley. Yield: 10 servings (½ cup per serving).

This recipe uses only one tablespoon of the **seasoning packet** to reduce sodium.

soups
&
sandwiches

Chilled Orange-Peach Soup

PREP: 11 minutes

Exchange
1 Fruit

POINTS
1

Per Serving
65 Calories
15.3g Carbohydrate
0.1g Fat (0.0g saturated)
0.7g Fiber
1.2g Protein
1mg Cholesterol
9mg Sodium
22mg Calcium
0.1mg Iron

1   (16-ounce) package frozen sliced peaches, partially thawed
¼   cup water
1½ cups unsweetened orange juice
½   cup peach nectar
½   cup vanilla nonfat yogurt
2   tablespoons honey
Fresh mint sprigs (optional)

1. Position knife blade in food processor bowl; add peaches and water. Process until smooth, stopping once to scrape down sides.

2. Pour peach mixture into a bowl. Add juice and next 3 ingredients; stir with a wire whisk until combined. Cover; chill until ready to serve. Garnish with mint, if desired. Yield: 10 servings (½ cup per serving).

> **Partially thaw peaches** in the microwave; just place them in a microwave-safe dish, and microwave at MEDIUM-LOW 6 minutes, stirring once.

Fresh Yellow Squash Soup (photo, page 174)

PREP: 6 minutes   COOK: 30 minutes

Vegetable cooking spray
1   cup chopped onion (about 1 medium onion)
1   teaspoon minced garlic (or 1 clove garlic, minced)
3   pounds yellow squash, cut into ¼-inch-thick slices
2   (16-ounce) cans reduced-sodium chicken broth
1   cup low-fat milk
¼   cup instant nonfat dry milk powder
3   ounces Neufchâtel cheese, cubed
1   teaspoon dried basil
½   teaspoon salt
¼   teaspoon pepper

1. Coat a Dutch oven with cooking spray; place over medium-high heat until hot. Add onion and garlic; sauté 5 minutes or until onion is tender. Add squash and chicken broth; bring to a boil. Cover, reduce heat, and simmer 15 to 20 minutes or until squash is tender, stirring occasionally.

2. Transfer mixture in batches to container of an electric blender or food processor; cover and process until mixture is smooth. Return puree to Dutch oven.

3. Combine milk and milk powder; add to pureed squash mixture. Stir in cheese and remaining ingredients. Cook soup over medium heat 10 minutes or until cheese is melted, stirring occasionally (do not boil). Yield: 9 servings (1 cup per serving).

Exchanges

2 Vegetable

½ Fat

POINTS

2

Per Serving

93 Calories

11.3g Carbohydrate

2.9g Fat (1.7g saturated)

2.7g Fiber

6.2g Protein

9mg Cholesterol

416mg Sodium

117mg Calcium

0.8mg Iron

When selecting yellow squash, be sure to look at the stem. If the stem is hard, shriveled, or darkened, the squash isn't fresh.

Spicy Tomato Florentine Soup (photo, page 174)

PREP: 5 minutes   COOK: 20 minutes

Exchanges
1 Starch
1 Vegetable
½ Fat

POINTS
2

Per Serving
125 Calories
23.4g Carbohydrate
2.2g Fat (0.2g saturated)
3.9g Fiber
3.9g Protein
0mg Cholesterol
651mg Sodium
70mg Calcium
1.2mg Iron

Vegetable cooking spray
1   teaspoon vegetable oil
¾   cup chopped onion (about 1 small onion)
1   clove garlic, minced
1½ cups water
1   (10-ounce) package frozen chopped spinach
2   (10¾-ounce) cans reduced-fat, reduced-sodium tomato soup, undiluted
1   (10-ounce) can diced tomatoes and green chiles, undrained
½   teaspoon pepper
½   cup fat-free croutons

1. Coat a large saucepan with cooking spray, and add oil. Place over medium-high heat until hot. Add onion and garlic; sauté 3 minutes or until onion is tender.

2. Add water and frozen spinach; bring to a boil. Cover, reduce heat, and simmer 10 minutes, stirring occasionally.

3. Add soup, tomatoes and green chiles, and pepper; bring to a boil. Cover, reduce heat, and simmer 5 minutes.

4. Ladle soup into individual soup bowls; top servings evenly with croutons. Yield: 6 servings (1 cup per serving).

Save time when preparing this recipe by adding the entire unthawed package of spinach straight to the pan.

Lentil Minestrone

PREP: 10 minutes   COOK: 20 minutes

2   (16-ounce) cans reduced-sodium chicken broth
¾   cup dried red lentils
2   ounces small shell pasta, uncooked
2   large carrots, thinly sliced
1   (14½-ounce) can diced tomatoes, undrained
½   cup frozen English peas
2   teaspoons dried basil
¼   teaspoon dried crushed red pepper

1. Combine first 4 ingredients in a medium saucepan; bring to a boil. Cover, reduce heat, and simmer 15 minutes.

2. Add tomatoes and remaining ingredients; bring to a boil. Reduce heat, and simmer, uncovered, 5 minutes or until lentils and carrot are tender. Yield: 7 servings (1 cup per serving).

Red lentils (actually bright orange) have a delightful peppery flavor. Look for them in the rice and dried bean section of your supermarket. You can substitute green or brown lentils.

Exchanges
½ Very Lean Meat
1½ Starch
½ Vegetable

POINTS
2

Per Serving
139 Calories
24.1g Carbohydrate
0.5g Fat (0.1g saturated)
3.0g Fiber
9.8g Protein
0mg Cholesterol
390mg Sodium
40mg Calcium
2.6mg Iron

Southwestern Chicken and Rice Soup

PREP: 5 minutes   COOK: 25 minutes

Exchanges

1½ Very Lean Meat

½ Starch

1 Vegetable

POINTS

2

Per Serving

117 Calories

14.6g Carbohydrate

1.2g Fat (0.3g saturated)

0.7g Fiber

11.1g Protein

23mg Cholesterol

395mg Sodium

11mg Calcium

1.0mg Iron

2   (16-ounce) cans reduced-sodium chicken broth

1   cup water

1   cup frozen onion, celery, and pepper seasoning blend

½   cup long-grain rice, uncooked

¼   teaspoon ground cumin

1½ cups chopped cooked chicken breast

1   cup peeled, seeded, and chopped tomato (about 1 large tomato)

½   cup frozen whole-kernel corn

1   (4.5-ounce) can chopped green chiles, undrained

¼   cup lime juice

2   tablespoons chopped fresh cilantro

¼   teaspoon salt

1. Bring broth and water to a boil in a large saucepan. Stir in seasoning blend, rice, and cumin. Return to a boil. Cover, reduce heat, and simmer 15 minutes or until rice is tender.

2. Stir chicken and next 3 ingredients into rice mixture; bring to a boil. Remove mixture from heat; stir in lime juice, cilantro, and salt. Yield: 8 servings (1 cup per serving).

Cook chicken quickly by bringing 1 cup water to a boil in a large skillet. Reduce heat to low, and add chicken breast halves. Cover and simmer 15 minutes or until done, turning chicken after 8 minutes. Two 4-ounce skinned, boned chicken breast halves will yield 1½ cups chopped cooked chicken.

Alphabet Vegetable-Beef Soup

PREP: 5 minutes   **COOK:** 25 minutes

1   pound ground chuck

2   cups low-sodium vegetable juice cocktail

2   (16-ounce) packages frozen vegetable soup mix with tomatoes

2   (14¼-ounce) cans no-salt-added beef broth

2   (14½-ounce) cans no-salt-added diced tomatoes, undrained

½   cup alphabet-shaped pasta, uncooked

1½   teaspoons salt

1   teaspoon dried Italian seasoning

½   teaspoon pepper

1. Cook ground chuck in a Dutch oven over medium heat until browned, stirring until it crumbles. Drain and pat dry with paper towels. Wipe drippings from Dutch oven with a paper towel.

2. Return beef to Dutch oven. Add juice cocktail and next 3 ingredients; bring mixture to a boil. Cover, reduce heat, and simmer 10 minutes. Add pasta and remaining ingredients to Dutch oven; bring to a boil. Cover, reduce heat, and simmer 10 minutes or until pasta is done. Yield: 14 servings (1 cup per serving).

Exchanges

1 Medium-Fat Meat

1 Starch

POINTS

3

Per Serving

144 Calories

16.6g Carbohydrate

4.6g Fat (1.8g saturated)

3.2g Fiber

8.9g Protein

19mg Cholesterol

346mg Sodium

9mg Calcium

0.8mg Iron

Picadillo-Style Chili

PREP: 10 minutes   COOK: 14 minutes

Exchanges
2 Lean Meat
2 Starch

POINTS
5

Per Serving
285 Calories
32.4g Carbohydrate
8.3g Fat (2.8g saturated)
8.7g Fiber
21.9g Protein
48mg Cholesterol
555mg Sodium
50mg Calcium
2.0mg Iron

¾ pound lean ground pork (or ground beef or ground turkey)
1 cup chopped onion (about 1 medium onion)
1½ teaspoons minced garlic
1 tablespoon chili powder
¼ teaspoon ground cinnamon
1 (15-ounce) can no-salt-added black beans, drained
1 (14½-ounce) can chili-style chunky tomatoes, undrained
1 green pepper, coarsely chopped
½ cup salsa
⅓ cup raisins

1. Place a large nonstick saucepan over medium-high heat until hot. Add ground pork, onion, and garlic; sauté 5 minutes or until pork is browned and onion is tender, stirring until pork crumbles. Drain well.

2. Return pork mixture to pan. Sprinkle with chili powder and cinnamon; cook over medium-high heat, stirring constantly, 1 minute.

3. Add black beans and remaining ingredients to pan; bring mixture to a boil. Reduce heat, and simmer, uncovered, 5 minutes, stirring occasionally. Yield: 5 servings (1 cup per serving).

Picadillo is a traditional dish of many Spanish-speaking countries. It usually consists of ground pork combined with either ground beef or veal, plus tomatoes, garlic, and onions. Here ground pork replaces the usual combination of ground meat, and the raisins and cinnamon add a slightly sweet taste.

Garden Pocket Pitas

PREP: 15 minutes

4   cups shredded romaine lettuce
1   cup diced cucumber
½   cup sliced green onions
1   (15.5-ounce) can garbanzo beans, drained
½   cup fat-free Italian dressing
1   tablespoon red wine vinegar
1   teaspoon Dijon mustard
4   (8-inch) whole wheat pita rounds (or regular pita rounds), cut in half crosswise
16   thin slices tomato (about 4 small tomatoes)
16   green pepper rings (about 3 small green peppers)
8   (1-ounce) slices Provolone cheese

Exchanges
1 High-Fat Meat
2 Starch
1 Vegetable

POINTS
5

Per Serving
299 Calories
38.3g Carbohydrate
9.7g Fat (5.0g saturated)
6.9g Fiber
13.6g Protein
20mg Cholesterol
611mg Sodium
283mg Calcium
3.3mg Iron

1. Combine first 4 ingredients. Combine dressing, vinegar, and mustard, mixing well. Pour over lettuce mixture. Toss well.

2. Spoon lettuce mixture evenly into pita halves. Place 2 tomato slices, 2 pepper rings, and 1 slice cheese over lettuce mixture in each pita half. Serve immediately. Yield: 8 servings.

Teriyaki Turkey Burgers (photo, page 2)

PREP: 13 minutes   COOK: 12 minutes

Exchanges

3 Very Lean Meat

2½ Starch

POINTS

5

Per Serving

283 Calories

36.8g Carbohydrate

2.7g Fat (0.6g saturated)

5.6g Fiber

31.1g Protein

68mg Cholesterol

930mg Sodium

31mg Calcium

1.8mg Iron

¼   cup reduced-sodium teriyaki sauce, divided

1   tablespoon brown sugar

6   slices canned pineapple, drained

½   cup ketchup

2   tablespoons hoisin sauce

1½ pounds ground turkey breast

Vegetable cooking spray

6   reduced-calorie whole wheat hamburger buns

6   lettuce leaves

1. Combine 1 tablespoon teriyaki sauce and brown sugar; brush over pineapple slices. Set aside. Combine ketchup and hoisin sauce.

2. Combine remaining 3 tablespoons teriyaki sauce, 2 tablespoons ketchup mixture, and turkey. Shape turkey mixture into 6 patties.

3. Coat grill rack with cooking spray; place on grill over medium-hot coals (350° to 400°). Place patties on rack; grill, covered, 6 minutes on each side or until done. Remove from grill; set aside, and keep warm.

4. Place pineapple on rack; grill, covered, 2 minutes on each side.

5. Spoon about 1½ tablespoons remaining ketchup mixture onto bottom half of each bun. Top each with a patty, a lettuce leaf, and a pineapple slice. Cover with top bun halves. Yield: 6 servings.

Find **hoisin sauce** in the Asian section of the supermarket. Or make your own: Just mix 3 tablespoons brown sugar, 3 tablespoons reduced-sodium soy sauce, and ¼ teaspoon garlic powder.

French Dip Sandwiches

PREP: 5 minutes   COOK: 5 minutes

1   (14¼-ounce) can no-salt-added beef broth
2   teaspoons dried onion flakes
4   small soft hoagie rolls, split lengthwise and toasted
1   tablespoon plus 1 teaspoon Dijon mustard
½   pound 98% fat-free thinly sliced deli roast beef

1. Place broth and onion flakes in a small saucepan; bring to a boil. Meanwhile, spread 1 side of rolls evenly with mustard.

2. Using tongs, dip one-fourth of beef slices into broth for 30 seconds. Repeat procedure with remaining roast beef. Place roast beef on bottom halves of rolls, and cover with top halves. Pour remaining broth into ramekins; serve with sandwiches. Yield: 4 servings.

The basic sandwich—bread, lunch meats, cheese, and mustard—can pile on the sodium. Fat-free meats and reduced-calorie condiments help slash fat and calories, but not sodium. Choose low-sodium accompaniments like carrot and celery sticks rather than chips or pickles.

Exchanges
1½ Lean Meat
2 Starch

POINTS
6

Per Serving
279 Calories
34.9g Carbohydrate
5.9g Fat (3.0g saturated)
2.1g Fiber
17.3g Protein
20mg Cholesterol
1053mg Sodium
23mg Calcium
0.7mg Iron

Greek Wraps (photo, opposite page)

PREP: 12 minutes   COOK: 8 minutes

Exchanges

1 Medium-Fat Meat

1½ Starch

POINTS

3

Per Serving

202 Calories

25.1g Carbohydrate

6.4g Fat (1.7g saturated)

6.2g Fiber

11.5g Protein

20mg Cholesterol

289mg Sodium

71mg Calcium

2.3mg Iron

Vegetable cooking spray

8   ounces lean ground round

½   cup chopped onion (about ½ medium onion)

2   cups hot cooked rice (cooked without salt or fat)

½   cup plain low-fat yogurt

¼   cup pine nuts, toasted

¼   cup reduced-fat feta cheese

1   tablespoon lemon juice

½   teaspoon garlic salt

¼   teaspoon pepper

⅛   to ¼ teaspoon ground cinnamon

4   (8-inch) flour tortillas

16   fresh spinach leaves (about 1½ ounces)

1. Coat a large skillet with cooking spray; place over medium-high heat until hot. Add ground round and onion; sauté 5 minutes or until beef is browned and onion is tender, stirring until beef crumbles. Drain well.

2. Combine beef mixture, rice, and next 7 ingredients; stir well. Lay tortillas on a flat surface; line with spinach leaves. Spread beef mixture evenly over tortillas; roll up tortillas, jellyroll fashion. Wrap in aluminum foil; cut in half to serve. Yield: 8 servings.

It's a wrap. Roll up your favorite sandwich ingredients in a flour tortilla. Then wrap in foil, wax paper, or a napkin, and you'll have today's version of the sandwich—a wrap.

**Spicy Tomato
Florentine Soup**
(recipe, page 164)

Fresh Yellow Squash Soup
(recipe, page 163)

Frozen Cherry Salad
(recipe, page 187)

**Sweet-and-Tangy
Marinated Slaw**
(recipe, page 185)

make-ahead recipes

Make-Ahead Magic

Make-ahead recipes are an easy way to save time, maximize flavor, and satisfy a hungry family. That's why we've dedicated a whole chapter to recipes that give you a jump start on dinner. Choose a time convenient for you—in the morning, during a child's nap, or at night—to spend a few minutes combining ingredients. Then marinate, chill, or freeze the recipe according to the directions. This "hands-off" time allows the flavors to develop and makes the recipe especially convenient for you. All you'll have left to do at dinnertime is grill, bake, or broil before serving up a tasty meal.

This chapter offers entrée, salad, and dessert recipes designed for your convenience. Tempting Beef Tenderloin with Horseradish Cream Sauce, refreshing Sweet-and-Tangy Marinated Slaw, and frosty Cool Lemon Pie are just a few of the make-ahead recipes you'll find. Let these recipes work for you by taking the worry and pressure out of cooking at a moment's notice. When your family is ready to eat, you'll have a satisfying meal at your fingertips—just like magic.

Mexican Casserole

PREP: 15 minutes   CHILL: 8 hours   COOK: 35 minutes

1	pound ground round
½	cup chopped onion (about ½ medium onion)
2	cloves garlic, minced
3	cups cooked rice (cooked without salt or fat)
¼	cup sliced ripe olives
2	tablespoons chopped fresh cilantro
1	(28-ounce) can tomatoes, undrained and chopped
1	(4.5-ounce) can chopped green chiles, undrained
1	(1¼-ounce) package 40%-less-sodium taco seasoning mix

Vegetable cooking spray

¾	cup (3 ounces) reduced-fat Monterey Jack cheese

Exchanges

3 Lean Meat

1½ Starch

1 Vegetable

POINTS

8

Per Serving

358 Calories

37.6g Carbohydrate

12.7g Fat (5.3g saturated)

2.1g Fiber

22.9g Protein

56mg Cholesterol

771mg Sodium

173mg Calcium

3.4mg Iron

1. Cook first 3 ingredients in a large skillet over medium-high heat until beef is browned, stirring until it crumbles; drain and return to skillet. Stir in rice and next 5 ingredients. Bring to a boil; reduce heat, and simmer, uncovered, 10 minutes. Spoon mixture into a 2-quart baking dish coated with cooking spray. Cover and chill 8 hours or overnight.

2. Bake casserole, uncovered, at 350° for 30 minutes or until thoroughly heated. Sprinkle with cheese, and bake 5 additional minutes or until cheese melts. Yield: 6 servings.

Turn this recipe into a **30-minute, one-dish meal** start to finish. Follow directions in step 1, but leave the beef-and-rice mixture in the skillet. After it simmers 10 minutes as directed, sprinkle with cheese; simmer 5 additional minutes or until mixture is thoroughly heated and cheese is melted.

Beef Tenderloin with Horseradish Cream Sauce

PREP: 7 minutes   MARINATE: 8 hours   COOK: 6 minutes

Exchanges
3 Lean Meat

POINTS
5

Per Serving
193 Calories
1.9g Carbohydrate
8.3g Fat (3.2g saturated)
0.1g Fiber
25.7g Protein
73mg Cholesterol
155mg Sodium
12mg Calcium
3.3mg Iron

Horseradish Cream Sauce received our highest flavor rating. For variety, serve it with pork or chicken—a tablespoon of sauce has only five calories.

½   cup nonfat sour cream
2   tablespoons prepared horseradish
¾   teaspoon white wine Worcestershire sauce
⅛   teaspoon salt
⅛   teaspoon pepper
¼   cup red wine vinegar
1   teaspoon chopped fresh thyme (or ½ teaspoon dried thyme)
¼   teaspoon pepper
4   (4-ounce) beef tenderloin steaks (about 1 inch thick)
Vegetable cooking spray
Fresh thyme sprigs (optional)

1. Combine first 5 ingredients. Cover Horseradish Cream Sauce, and chill 8 hours or overnight.

2. Combine vinegar, chopped thyme, and ¼ teaspoon pepper in a large heavy-duty, zip-top plastic bag. Add steaks; seal bag, and shake until meat is well coated. Marinate steaks in refrigerator 8 hours or overnight, turning bag occasionally.

3. Remove steaks from marinade, discarding marinade. Place steaks on rack of a broiler pan coated with cooking spray. Broil 3 inches from heat (with electric oven door partially opened) 3 to 4 minutes on each side or to desired degree of doneness.

4. Place steaks on four individual serving plates; serve each steak with 2½ tablespoons Horseradish Cream Sauce. Garnish with thyme sprigs, if desired. Yield: 4 servings.

Grilled Pork Teriyaki

PREP: 5 minutes   **MARINATE:** 8 hours   **COOK:** 25 minutes

2   (¾-pound) pork tenderloins
½   cup low-sodium soy sauce
¼   cup unsweetened orange juice
¼   cup unsweetened pineapple juice
2   tablespoons brown sugar
1   tablespoon peeled, grated gingerroot
2   cloves garlic, minced
Vegetable cooking spray

1. Place pork in a large heavy-duty, zip-top plastic bag. Combine soy sauce and next 5 ingredient; pour over pork. Seal bag; marinate in refrigerator 8 hours or overnight, turning bag occasionally.

2. Remove pork from marinade, discarding marinade. Coat grill rack with cooking spray; place on grill over medium-hot coals (350° to 400°). Place pork on rack; grill, covered, 25 to 30 minutes or until meat thermometer inserted in thickest portion of pork registers 160°, turning occasionally. Yield: 6 servings.

Exchanges
3 Very Lean Meat
½ Starch

POINTS
4

Per Serving
181 Calories
6.0g Carbohydrate
4.4g Fat (1.5g saturated)
0.1g Fiber
25.9g Protein
83mg Cholesterol
581mg Sodium
15mg Calcium
1.5mg Iron

Sausage Breakfast Casserole

PREP: 15 minutes   CHILL: 8 hours   COOK: 30 minutes

Exchanges
1½ Lean Meat
1 Starch

POINTS
3

Per Serving
156 Calories
15.7g Carbohydrate
4.4g Fat (1.9g saturated)
0.5g Fiber
13.0g Protein
16mg Cholesterol
450mg Sodium
205mg Calcium
1.3mg Iron

3 cups (1-inch) cubed French bread

Vegetable cooking spray

½ pound bulk turkey sausage (such as Louis Rich)

¼ cup chopped green onions (about 4 green onions)

¾ cup (3 ounces) shredded reduced-fat sharp Cheddar cheese

1 cup fat-free milk

1 cup egg substitute

½ teaspoon dry mustard

¼ teaspoon salt

¼ teaspoon pepper

1. Arrange bread cubes in an 11- x 7- x 1½-inch baking dish coated with cooking spray.

2. Coat a large nonstick skillet with cooking spray; place skillet over medium-high heat until hot. Add sausage and green onions; cook until sausage is browned, stirring until it crumbles. Drain, if necessary. Layer sausage mixture and cheese over bread cubes.

3. Combine milk and remaining 4 ingredients; pour over bread mixture, bread and cheese. Press down on bread mixture with a spatula to cover totally with milk mixture. Cover and chill 8 hours or overnight.

4. Bake casserole, uncovered, at 350° for 30 minutes or until set and lightly browned. Let stand 5 minutes before serving. Yield: 6 servings.

Turkey-Spaghetti Casserole

PREP: 20 minutes   CHILL: 8 hours   COOK: 35 minutes

8   ounces spaghetti, uncooked

Vegetable cooking spray

¾   cup chopped onion (about 1 small onion)

¾   cup chopped green pepper (about 1 small pepper)

¾   cup fat-free milk

½   teaspoon pepper

¼   teaspoon salt

1   (10¾-ounce) can reduced-sodium cream of chicken soup,
        undiluted

2   cups chopped cooked turkey breast

1   (4½-ounce) jar sliced mushrooms, drained

1   (4-ounce) jar diced pimiento, drained

1   cup (4 ounces) shredded reduced-fat sharp Cheddar cheese

1. Cook spaghetti according to package directions, omitting salt and fat. Drain.

2. Meanwhile, coat a Dutch oven with cooking spray; place over medium heat until hot. Add onion and green pepper; sauté 5 minutes or until tender.

3. Combine onion mixture, milk, and next 3 ingredients; stir well. Combine pasta, turkey, mushrooms, and pimiento; toss gently. Pour soup mixture over pasta mixture; toss until pasta is well coated.

4. Spoon mixture into an 11- x 7- x 1½-inch baking dish coated with cooking spray. Cover and chill 8 hours or overnight. Bake, uncovered, at 375° for 30 minutes. Sprinkle with cheese; bake, uncovered, 5 additional minutes or until cheese melts. Yield: 6 servings.

Exchanges

2 Lean Meat

2 Starch

1 Vegetable

POINTS

7

Per Serving

326 Calories

39.1g Carbohydrate

5.7g Fat (2.8g saturated)

1.6g Fiber

27.8g Protein

58mg Cholesterol

567mg Sodium

225mg Calcium

2.9mg Iron

Skip the chill step, if desired. Just assemble the casserole; then bake at 375° for 10 minutes. Sprinkle with cheese; bake 5 more minutes or until cheese melts.

Marinated Bean Salad

PREP: 12 minutes   COOK: 2 minutes   CHILL: 8 hours

Exchanges
1 Starch
1 Vegetable

POINTS
2

Per Serving
118 Calories
26.2g Carbohydrate
0.4g Fat (0.1g saturated)
4.0g Fiber
4.5g Protein
0mg Cholesterol
471mg Sodium
45mg Calcium
2.1mg Iron

1   (15½-ounce) can dark red kidney beans, rinsed and drained
1   (15¼-ounce) can lima beans, drained
1   (14½-ounce) can no-salt-added cut green beans, drained
1   (14½-ounce) can cut wax beans, drained
1   cup chopped sweet red or green pepper (about 1 large pepper)
1   cup chopped purple onion (about ½ large onion)
1   cup chopped celery (about 3 large stalks celery)
1   cup cider vinegar
⅓   cup sugar
½   teaspoon garlic powder
½   teaspoon salt
½   teaspoon freshly ground pepper

1. Combine first 7 ingredients in a large bowl; set aside.

2. Combine vinegar and remaining 4 ingredients in a small saucepan; cook over medium-high heat until mixture comes to a boil and sugar dissolves, stirring occasionally. Pour hot vinegar mixture over bean mixture; toss gently to combine.

3. Cover and chill at least 8 hours, tossing occasionally. Serve with a slotted spoon. Yield: 8 servings (1 cup per serving).

Sweet-and-Tangy Marinated Slaw (photo, page 176)

PREP: 4 minutes   **COOK:** 2 minutes   **CHILL:** 8 hours

1   (16-ounce) package broccoli slaw
½   cup sugar
¼   cup cider vinegar
1   teaspoon prepared mustard
½   teaspoon celery seeds
¼   teaspoon salt
¼   teaspoon pepper
Additional pepper (optional)

1. Place broccoli slaw in a large bowl. Combine sugar and next 5 ingredients in a small saucepan; bring to a boil. Remove from heat; pour over slaw, and toss well.

2. Cover; chill 8 hours or overnight. Serve with a slotted spoon. Sprinkle with additional pepper, if desired. Yield: 5 servings (1 cup per serving).

Exchanges

½ Starch

2 Vegetable

POINTS

2

Per Serving

101 Calories

23.9g Carbohydrate

0.1g Fat (0.0g saturated)

1.1g Fiber

0.6g Protein

0mg Cholesterol

146mg Sodium

14mg Calcium

0.3mg Iron

Use **preshredded broccoli slaw mix,** found in the produce section of your supermarket, to get you out of the kitchen fast.

Marinated Tortellini Salad

PREP: 10 minutes   CHILL: 8 hours

Exchanges
1 Starch
1 Vegetable
1 Fat

POINTS
3

Per Serving
149 Calories
20.6g Carbohydrate
5.0g Fat (1.9g saturated)
2.0g Fiber
5.2g Protein
13mg Cholesterol
270mg Sodium
35mg Calcium
0.6mg Iron

1   (9-ounce) package refrigerated cheese-filled tortellini, uncooked
1½ cups broccoli flowerets
1   cup cauliflower flowerets
1   cup halved cherry tomatoes
1   medium-size green pepper, thinly sliced
1   small purple onion, thinly sliced
½   cup reduced-fat pesto-Parmesan salad dressing (such as Maple Grove Farms)

1. Cook pasta according to package directions, omitting salt and fat. Drain and rinse with cold water.

2. Combine pasta, broccoli, and next 4 ingredients in a large bowl. Add dressing, tossing gently to coat. Cover and chill 8 hours or overnight. Yield: 8 servings (1 cup per serving).

Jump-start this salad by purchasing broccoli and cauliflower flowerets. Both are available in 16-ounce bags in the produce section of your local supermarket. Or, find broccoli and cauliflower flowerets at the salad bar.

Frozen Cherry Salad (photo, page 175)

PREP: 8 minutes   FREEZE: 8 hours

1   (20-ounce) can reduced-calorie cherry pie filling
1   (14-ounce) can fat-free sweetened condensed milk
1   (8-ounce) can crushed pineapple in juice, drained
1   tablespoon lemon juice
1   (8-ounce) container frozen reduced-calorie whipped topping,
        thawed
Vegetable cooking spray

1. Combine first 4 ingredients; fold in whipped topping.

2. Coat an 8-inch square pan with cooking spray; pour cherry mixture into prepared pan. Cover and freeze 8 hours or overnight. Cut into rectangles. Yield: 10 servings.

You can serve this **dual-purpose recipe** as a creamy salad or a refreshing dessert.

Exchanges

1 Starch
2 Fruit
½ Fat

POINTS

4

Per Serving

217 Calories
43.4g Carbohydrate
3.0g Fat (3.0g saturated)
0.9g Fiber
3.7g Protein
0mg Cholesterol
65mg Sodium
17mg Calcium
0.0mg Iron

Cool Lemon Pie

PREP: 5 minutes   FREEZE: 8 hours

Exchanges
2 Starch
1 Fruit
½ Fat

POINTS
5

Per Serving
242 Calories
47.1g Carbohydrate
3.7g Fat (2.1g saturated)
0.1g Fiber
4.1g Protein
0mg Cholesterol
124mg Sodium
9mg Calcium
0.1mg Iron

1   (14-ounce) can fat-free sweetened condensed milk
1   (6-ounce) can frozen lemonade concentrate, thawed and undiluted
1½ cups frozen reduced-calorie whipped topping, thawed
1   (6-ounce) reduced-fat graham cracker crust
Lemon slices (optional)

1. Combine sweetened condensed milk and lemonade concentrate; fold in whipped topping. Pour mixture into crust. Cover and freeze 8 hours or overnight.

2. Cut pie into slices; place on individual serving plates. Garnish with lemon slices, if desired. Yield: 10 servings (1 slice per serving).

Recipe Index

Appetizers
  Dips
    Bean Artichoke Dip, Three-, 14
    Cheese-Bean Dip, Blue, 12
    Pepper and Onion Dip, Roasted Red, 13
    Spinach con Queso, 15
  Nachos, Mediterranean, 16
  Polenta Bites with Red Pepper Sauce, 17
  Rolls, Open-Faced Hawaiian Pork, 18
Apples
  Cake, Caramel-Apple, 49
  Muffins, Apple Butter-Bran, 26
  Picadillo, Turkey, 127
  Waldorf Pilaf, 160
Artichokes
  Couscous, Mediterranean, 153
  Dip, Three-Bean Artichoke, 14
  Salad, Mixed Antipasto, 136

Bacon-Cheese Drop Biscuits, 27
Bacon-Horseradish Dressing, Mixed Greens with, 135
Banana Pancakes, 37
Banana Pudding, Double-Chocolate, 46
Barbecue Burritos, 91
Barbecue Chopped Steaks, 92
Barley Skillet, Ham and, 105
Beans. See also Salads/Bean.
  Chili, Picadillo-Style, 168
  Chili, Twenty-Minute, 76
  Dip, Blue Cheese-Bean, 12
  Dip, Three-Bean Artichoke, 14
  Eggs, Mexican-Style Poached, 73
  Enchiladas, Vegetable-Bean, 74
  Green Beans, Mustard Potatoes and, 147
  Nachos, Mediterranean, 16
  Peppers, Tuscan-Style, 82
  Pitas, Garden Pocket, 169
  Tostadas, Beef and Bean, 90
  Turkey Skillet, Santa Fe, 125
  Wraps, Corn and Bean, 75
Beef
  Sandwiches, French Dip, 171
  Steak au Poivre, 94
  Steaks with Mushroom Sauce, Savory, 96
  Stir-Fry, Gingered Beef, 95
  Tenderloin with Horseradish Cream Sauce,
    Beef, 180

Beef, Ground
  Burritos, Barbecue, 91
  Casserole, Mexican, 179
  Chopped Steaks, Barbecue, 92
  Pie, Speedy Shepherd's, 93
  Soup, Alphabet Vegetable-Beef, 167
  Tostadas, Beef and Bean, 90
  Wraps, Greek, 172
Beverages
  Mix, Mocha Cocoa, 24
  Shake, Mocha Cocoa, 24
  Shakes, Piña Colada Milk, 54
  Shakes, Strawberry-Piña Colada Milk, 54
  Slush, Sunrise, 20
  Smoothie, Blueberry, 23
  Tea, Lemonade-Mint Iced, 19
Biscuits
  Bacon-Cheese Drop Biscuits, 27
  Cheese Biscuits, Cream, 29
  Cinnamon-Raisin Biscuits, 28
  Sage Biscuits, Turkey Stroganoff on, 129
Blueberry-Lemon Cheesecake Parfaits, 43
Blueberry Smoothie, 23
Bran Muffins, Apple Butter-, 26
Breads. See also Biscuits.
  Cheese Bread, Peppered Pimiento, 33
  Cornbread, Chipotle Chile, 38
  Crescents, Broccoli-Cheddar, 34
  Danish, Strawberry-Almond, 35
  Flatbread, Tomato-Parmesan, 32
  French Toast, Raisin Bread, 36
  Muffins, Apple Butter-Bran, 26
  Pancakes, Banana, 37
  Rolls, Light Mayonnaise, 31
  Scones, Sweet Potato, 30
Broccoli
  Cheese Sauce, Broccoli with Caraway-, 148
  Crescents, Broccoli-Cheddar, 34
  Potatoes, Broccoli-Cheddar, 87
  Slaw, Sweet-and-Tangy Marinated, 185
Brownie Bites, Fudgy-Mint, 51
Burritos, Barbecue, 91

Cabbage
  Burritos, Barbecue, 91
  Slaw, Chunky Asian, 139
  Wraps, Corn and Bean, 75

Cakes
    Caramel-Apple Cake, 49
    Chocolate Pudding Cake, Easy, 50
    Hummingbird Loaf Cake, 48
    Shortcakes, Fruit-Filled Chocolate, 45
    Shortcakes, Pineapple-Coconut, 44
Carrots and Celery, Lemon-Dill, 149
Casseroles
    Mexican Casserole, 179
    Potato Casserole, Sweet, 150
    Sausage Breakfast Casserole, 182
    Turkey-Spaghetti Casserole, 183
Cheese
    Biscuits, Bacon-Cheese Drop, 27
    Biscuits, Cream Cheese, 29
    Bread, Peppered Pimiento Cheese, 33
    Crescents, Broccoli-Cheddar, 34
    Dip, Blue Cheese-Bean, 12
    Flatbread, Tomato-Parmesan, 32
    Grits, Garlic-Cheese, 154
    Orzo and Peas, Parmesan, 158
    Pizza, Roasted Vegetable, 88
    Potatoes, Broccoli-Cheddar, 87
    Sauce, Broccoli with Caraway-Cheese, 148
    Spinach con Queso, 15
    Tomatoes, Cheese-Stuffed, 152
Cherry-Chocolate Turnovers, Baked, 52
Cherry Salad, Frozen, 187
Chicken
    Dijon Chicken Strips, Herbed, 110
    Dumplings, Chicken and, 123
    Greek Chicken with Lemon Couscous, 115
    Grilled Chicken, Rosemary-, 113
    Lemon Chicken, Saucy, 114
    Mushroom Sauce, Chicken with, 121
    Peach Sauce, Chicken with Spiced, 116
    Rice, Fiesta Chicken and, 112
    Salad, Spicy Chicken Finger, 144
    Soup, Southwestern Chicken and Rice, 166
    Sweet-and-Sour Chicken, 111
    Tropical Grilled Chicken, 122
Chili, Picadillo-Style, 168
Chili, Twenty-Minute, 76
Chocolate. *See also* Brownie.
    Cake, Easy Chocolate Pudding, 50
    Mix, Mocha Cocoa, 24
    Mousse, Creamy Mocha-Almond, 47
    Pudding, Double-Chocolate Banana, 46
    Shake, Mocha Cocoa, 24
    Shortcakes, Fruit-Filled Chocolate, 45
    Turnovers, Baked Cherry-Chocolate, 52
Clam Sauce, Linguine with Red, 69
Coconut Shortcakes, Pineapple-, 44

Corn and Bean Wraps, 75
Corn Relish, Peppered Pork with, 101
Couscous
    Lamb Chops, Middle Eastern, 106
    Lemon Couscous, Greek Chicken with, 115
    Mediterranean Couscous, 153
    Tomatoes, Couscous-Stuffed, 83
    Vegetable Couscous, Curried, 84
Cucumber Salad, Minted Melon-, 132

Desserts. *See also* Brownie, Cakes, Pie, Parfaits.
    Custard, Fresh Strawberries with Lime, 42
    Gingersnap-Date Balls, 53
    Mousse, Creamy Mocha-Almond, 47
    Pudding, Double-Chocolate Banana, 46
    Turnovers, Baked Cherry-Chocolate, 52

Eggs, Mexican-Style Poached, 73
Enchiladas, Vegetable-Bean, 74

Fish
    Catfish Nuggets with Tartar Sauce, 56
    Grouper, Cajun, 62
    Grouper, Herb-Crusted, 61
    Halibut Provençal, 63
    Salmon, Grilled Glazed, 64
    Snapper, Garlic-Baked, 66
    Snapper with Garlic-Cilantro Sauce, 65
    Tuna Steaks, Asian, 68
    Tuna Steaks, Chipotle-Chutney, 67
Frittata, Spinach, 72
Fruit. *See also* specific types.
    Salad, Minted Melon-Cucumber, 132
    Salad, Tropical Fruit, 133
    Shortcakes, Fruit-Filled Chocolate, 45

Grits, Garlic-Cheese, 154

Ham and Barley Skillet, 105

Kabobs, Hoisin-Grilled Shrimp, 70

Lamb Chops, Middle Eastern, 106
Lemon
    Carrots and Celery, Lemon-Dill, 149
    Chicken, Saucy Lemon, 114

Couscous, Greek Chicken with Lemon, 115
Parfaits, Blueberry-Lemon Cheesecake, 43
Pie, Cool Lemon, 188
Tea, Lemonade-Mint Iced, 19
Lentil Minestrone, 165
Lime Custard, Fresh Strawberries with, 42

Mushroom Sauce, Chicken with, 121
Mushroom Sauce, Savory Steaks with, 96

Onion Dip, Roasted Red Pepper and, 13
Onions, Pork Medaillons with Glazed, 103
Orange-Peach Soup, Chilled, 162
Orzo and Peas, Parmesan, 158

Parfaits, Blueberry-Lemon Cheesecake, 43
Pastas
    Linguine with Red Clam Sauce, 69
    Minestrone, Lentil, 165
    Peanut Pasta, Spicy, 157
    Salad, Marinated Tortellini, 186
    Salad, Vegetable-Tortellini, 143
    Sausage and Vegetables, Pasta with, 130
    Spaghetti Casserole, Turkey-, 183
    Turkey, Peppers, and Basil with Pasta, 126
Peach Sauce, Chicken with Spiced, 116
Peach Soup, Chilled Orange-, 162
Pears, Gingered, 146
Peas
    Black-Eyed Peas, Rice with, 159
    Minestrone, Lentil, 165
    Orzo and Peas, Parmesan, 158
    Slaw, Chunky Asian, 139
    Stir-Fry, Szechuan Pork, 104
    Tomatoes, Couscous-Stuffed, 83
Peppers
    Chile Cornbread, Chipotle, 38
    Dip, Roasted Red Pepper and Onion, 13
    Pasta, Turkey, Peppers, and Basil with, 126
    Roasted Squash and Peppers, 151
    Sauce, Polenta Bites with Red Pepper, 17
    Tuscan-Style Peppers, 82
Pie, Cool Lemon, 188
Pineapple
    Cake, Hummingbird Loaf, 48
    Kabobs, Hoisin-Grilled Shrimp, 70
    Shakes, Piña Colada Milk, 54
    Shakes, Strawberry-Piña Colada Milk, 54
    Shortcakes, Pineapple-Coconut, 44
    Turkey Burgers, Teriyaki, 170

Pitas, Garden Pocket, 169
Pizza, Roasted Vegetable, 88
Polenta Bites with Red Pepper Sauce, 17
Polenta with Roasted Vegetables, Creamy, 81
Pork
    Chili, Picadillo-Style, 168
    Chops, Spicy-Sweet Pork, 102
    Medaillons with Glazed Onions, Pork, 103
    Peppered Pork with Corn Relish, 101
    Rolls, Open-Faced Hawaiian Pork, 18
    Stir-Fry, Szechuan Pork, 104
    Teriyaki, Grilled Pork, 181
Potatoes. *See also* Sweet Potato.
    Broccoli-Cheddar Potatoes, 87
    Mustard Potatoes and Green Beans, 147
    Pie, Speedy Shepherd's, 93
    Salad, Creamy Mustard-Dill Potato, 140
    Turkey Hash, Old-Fashioned, 128

Raisin Biscuits, Cinnamon-, 28
Raisin Bread French Toast, 36
Rice
    Brown Rice with Vegetable Sauté, 85
    Chicken and Rice, Fiesta, 112
    Peas, Rice with Black-Eyed, 159
    Pilaf, Waldorf, 160
    Salad, Black Bean-Rice, 141
    Soup, Southwestern Chicken and Rice, 166

Salads
    Bean
        Marinated Bean Salad, 184
        Rice Salad, Black Bean-, 141
        Spinach Salad, Greek, 134
        Vegetarian Taco Salad, 142
    Cherry Salad, Frozen, 187
    Chicken Finger Salad, Spicy, 144
    Fruit Salad, Tropical, 133
    Greens with Bacon-Horseradish Dressing,
        Mixed, 135
    Melon-Cucumber Salad, Minted, 132
    Mixed Antipasto Salad, 136
    Potato Salad, Creamy Mustard-Dill, 140
    Slaw, Chunky Asian, 139
    Slaw, Sweet-and-Tangy Marinated, 185
    Tortellini Salad, Marinated, 186
    Tortellini Salad, Vegetable-, 143
Sandwiches. *See also* Pitas.
    French Dip Sandwiches, 171
    Turkey Burgers, Teriyaki, 170
    Wraps, Greek, 172

Sausage and Vegetables, Pasta with, 130
Sausage Breakfast Casserole, 182
Seafood. See Clam, Fish, Shrimp.
Shrimp Kabobs, Hoisin-Grilled, 70
Soups. See also Chili.
    Chicken and Rice Soup, Southwestern, 166
    Minestrone, Lentil, 165
    Orange-Peach Soup, Chilled, 162
    Squash Soup, Fresh Yellow, 163
    Tomato Florentine Soup, Spicy, 164
    Vegetable-Beef Soup, Alphabet, 167
Spinach
    con Queso, Spinach, 15
    Frittata, Spinach, 72
    Salad, Greek Spinach, 134
    Soup, Spicy Tomato Florentine, 164
    Wraps, Greek, 172
Squash and Peppers, Roasted, 151
Squash Soup, Fresh Yellow, 163
Strawberries
    Custard, Fresh Strawberries with Lime, 42
    Danish, Strawberry-Almond, 35
    Shakes, Strawberry-Piña Colada Milk, 54
    Smoothie, Blueberry, 23
Stroganoff on Sage Biscuits, Turkey, 129
Sweet Potato Casserole, 150
Sweet Potato Scones, 30

Taco Salad, Vegetarian, 142
Tofu
    Stir-Fry, Asian Vegetable, 86
Tomatoes
    Flatbread, Tomato-Parmesan, 32
    Soup, Spicy Tomato Florentine, 164

Stuffed Tomatoes, Cheese-, 152
Stuffed Tomatoes, Couscous-, 83
Tortillas. See also Burritos, Enchiladas, Taco.
    Eggs, Mexican-Style Poached, 73
    Tostadas, Beef and Bean, 90
    Wraps, Corn and Bean, 75
    Wraps, Greek, 172
Turkey
    Burgers, Teriyaki Turkey, 170
    Casserole, Turkey-Spaghetti, 183
    Chutney Glaze, Turkey with, 124
    Hash, Old-Fashioned Turkey, 128
    Pasta, Turkey, Peppers, and Basil with, 126
    Picadillo, Turkey, 127
    Skillet, Santa Fe Turkey, 125
    Stroganoff on Sage Biscuits, Turkey, 129

Veal Chops, Rosemary-Grilled, 107
Veal Cutlets Paprikash, 108
Vegetables. See also specific types.
    Chicken and Dumplings, 123
    Chili, Twenty-Minute, 76
    Couscous, Curried Vegetable, 84
    Enchiladas, Vegetable-Bean, 74
    Pasta with Sausage and Vegetables, 130
    Pitas, Garden Pocket, 169
    Pizza, Roasted Vegetable, 88
    Polenta with Roasted Vegetables, Creamy, 81
    Salad, Marinated Tortellini, 186
    Salad, Vegetable-Tortellini, 143
    Sauté, Brown Rice with Vegetable, 85
    Soup, Alphabet Vegetable-Beef, 167
    Stir-Fry, Asian Vegetable, 86
    Stir-Fry, Gingered Beef, 95

Acknowledgments & Credits

Aletha Soulé, The Loom Co., New York, NY
Annieglass, Watsonville, CA
Carolyn Rice, Marietta, GA
Cyclamen Studio, Inc., Berkeley, CA
Daisy Hill, Louisville, KY
E&M Glass, Cheshire, UK
Eigen Arts, Inc., Jersey City, NJ
Fioriware, New York, NY
Jill Rosenwald, Boston, MA
Karen Alweil Studio, Westminster, CA
Mariposa, Manchester, MA
Mesolini, Bainbridge Island, WI

Pillivyt-Franmara, Salinas, CA
Smyer Glass, Benicia, CA
Union Street Glass, Oakland, CA
Vietri, Hillsborough, NC

Contributing photo stylist:
Leslie Byars Simpson: pages 2, 137, 155

Sources of Nutrient Analysis Data:
Computrition, Inc., Chatsworth, CA,
and information provided by food
manufacturers